THE DONALD TRUMP PAPERS

A Collection of Fairy Tales, Monster Myths,
Kids' Stories, Cartoons, Poems, and Commentary
about Trump's Improbable Campaign and Presidency

by Gini Graham Scott, Ph.D.

Author of over 200 published books, regular Huffington Post columnist, and chief contributor to the website:
www.trumpisnuts.net (aka: www.trumpisanut.com)

Copyright © 2017 by Gini Graham Scott

All rights reserved. No part of this book may be used or reproduced by any means, graphic, electronic, or mechanical, including photocopying, recording, taping or by any information storage retrieval system without the written permission of the author except in the case of brief quotations embodied in critical articles and reviews.

TABLE OF CONTENTS

INTRODUCTION 7
PART I: FAIRY TALES AND MYTHS.. 9
2016 ELECTION FAIRY TALES... 11
INTRODUCTION 13
CHAPTER 1: TWO FAIRY TALES ABOUT DONALD TRUMP 15
CHAPTER 2: SNOW WHITE AND THE SEVEN CANDIDATES..................... 19
CHAPTER 3: LITTLE RED RIDING HOOD AND THE BIG BAD TRUMP..... 23
CHAPTER 4: THE THREE LITTLE PIGS AND THE BIG BAD TRUMP 27
CHAPTER 5: GOLDITRUMP AND THE THREE BEARS 31
CHAPTER 6: HANSEL AND GRETEL AND THE GINGERTRUMP HOUSE.. 35
CHAPTER 7: CHICKEN LITTLE AND THE BOY WHO CRIED TRUMP...... 39
THE VERY GREAT MONSTER IN THE WHITE HOUSE 43
CHAPTER 1: TRUMP AND THE MONSTER MYTH MASH 45
CHAPTER 2: IS TRUMP A CHIMERA?... 49
CHAPTER 3: BEHEADING THE TRUMP CAMPAIGN 53
CHAPTER 4: COULD TRUMP BE THE U.S. CYCLOPS?.................................. 57
CHAPTER 5: BEWARE THE TRUMP WATER MONSTER 61
CHAPTER 6: TRUMP AND THE MONSTERS OF THE SEA 65
CHAPTER 7: TRUMP AND THE MANY HEADED MONSTERS 69
CHAPTER 8: TRUMP AND THE HUMAN BEASTS 73
CHAPTER 9: IS TRUMP THE MODERN-DAY DEVIL?.................................... 77
PART II: CHILDREN'S STORIES FOR ADULTS 81
THE BATTLES OF DONNIE AND TEDDY 83
INTRODUCTION 85
IN THE SANDBOX 87
AT THE BIRTHDAY PARTY.. 99
AT THE LAKE 113
AT THE PLAYGROUND 129
PART III: CARTOON BOOKS 147
TRUMP IS EXTINCT…OR MAY BE SOON!.. 149
INTRODUCTION 151
DINOSAURS... 153
    Trumposaurus 155
    Tryannosaurus Trump.. 157
    Trumporaptor 159
    Spinotrumpus 161
    Brontotrumpus 163

- Stegotrumpus 165
- Iguanoramos Trumpus 167
- Trumpatops 169
- Anklyotrumpus vs. Tyrannus Kasich 171
- Hadrotrumpus 173

FLYING REPTILES 175
- Trumpodactyl 177
- Quetzalotrumpus 179

MARINE REPTILES 181
- Mosatrumpus 183
- Pliotrumpus (maybe the Loch Ness Trump) 185

BIRDS 187
- Dodo Trump 189
- Giant Trump Terror Bird 191

MAMMALS 193
- Woolly Rhinotrump 195
- Giant Trump Sloth 197
- Saber Tooth Trump and Giant Cruz Sloth 199
- Mastotrump 201
- Woolly Trumpoth 203

EARLY APES AND HUMANS 205
- Gigantotrumpus 207
- Homo Trumpilis 209
- Trumpo Erectus 211
- Neandertrump 213
- Homo Trumpien 215
- Homo Trumpus Trumpus 217

THE EVOLUTION OF HUMANS 219

TRUMP IS NUTS! 221

INTRODUCTION 223

A WHOLE LOT OF NUTS 225
- Mixed Nuts 227
- It's a Nut Case 229
- A Bag of Nuts 231

POWER NUTS 233
- Trumpking Cashew Nut 235
- Trump Almond Power Bar 237
- Macadamia Nut (aka Military Nut) 239
- Trumpflower Seed 241
- Hickory Nuts 243

TOUGH NUTS 245

Wall-Nut	247
Southern Pecan	249
Just a Regular Cashew Nut	251
Trumpkin Seed	253
MONEY NUTS	**255**
Hazeltrump Nut	257
Trump Wingnut Special	259
VERY NUTTY NUTS	**261**
The Trump Coconut	263
Brazil Trumpnut	265
Pistachio Trumpnut	267
Nutty Nutmeg	269
Welcome to the Nut House	271
NO MORE NUTS	**273**
Fallen Acorn	275
Getting Down to the Nuts and Bolts	277
TRUMP IS AN ANIMAL!	**279**
INTRODUCTION	**281**
MAMMALS	**283**
Kicking Kangaroos	285
Cunning Coyotes	287
Chimp Champion	289
Baaad Ass Baboons	291
Trump Elephants	293
Huuuge Hippos	295
Republican Rhinos	297
Trumpalos	299
Trumphorn Sheep	301
Trump Elk	303
Battling Bears	305
A Losing Lion	307
Trump Fur Seal of Approval	309
Mighty Meerkats	311
BIRDS	**313**
Cock Fighting	315
Penguin Power	317
Eagle Power	319
REPTILES	**321**
Trump the Tortoise	323
Dueling Dragons	325
Snake Eyes	327

PART IV: POEMS 329
DEAR DONALD TRUMP, WHAT'S WRONG WITH THE FBI? 331
DEAR DONALD TRUMP, ARE WE GOING TO WAR? 361
PART V: COMMENTARY 405
TRUMPTY DUMPTY 407
INTRODUCTION 409
CHAPTER 1: WHY ISN'T TRUMP ATTACKING THE CARTOONISTS AND WRITERS WHO ARE ATTACKING HIM? 411
CHAPTER 2: WHY TRUMP IS LIKE A FIGHTING ANIMAL 415
CHAPTER 3: IS TRUMP REALLY NUTS? 417
CHAPTER 4: DOES TRUMP HAVE EARLY-STAGE ALZHEIMER'S? 421
CHAPTER 5: PRO-TRUMPERS RESPOND TO THE QUESTION: "DOES TRUMP HAVE EARLY- STAGE ALZHEIMER'S?" 425
CHAPTER 6: TRUMP IS A NUT WEBSITE ECHOES VIEW OF REPUBLICAN INSIDER 429
CHAPTER 7: THE NAKED TRUMP STATUES SHOW TRUMP'S TRUE NATURE 431
ABOUT THE AUTHOR AND ILLUSTRATOR 433

INTRODUCTION

Following are a series of books I wrote about Donald Trump beginning in February 2016. They began with a single column I wrote for the *Huffington Post,* in which I featured two fairy tales where I compared Trump and his then unlikely campaign for President to "The Emperor Has No Clothes" and "The Pied Piper of Hamlin." I wrote this column because dozens of journalists and commentators were already commenting on how Trump was affecting the election, and a news broadcaster working part-time for me suggested I write something, too. But what? I didn't want to write what others were saying, so the fairy tale idea came to me.

After I wrote my first column, I began thinking about how Trump fit into other fairy tales as the big bad wolf character, and that led to a series of modern day updates of traditional tales, such as "Little Red Riding Hood and the Big Bad Trump," "The Three Little Pigs and the Big Bad Trump," and "The Boy Who Cried Trump."

Then, working with fairy tales led me to think about how Trump might be like some mythological characters, resulting in stories such as, "Could Trump Be the U.S. Cyclops," "Trump and the Many Headed Monsters," and "Is Trump a Chimera?"

After that, Trump's yelling and screaming battles with Ted Cruz led me to write four children's stories for adults called *The Battles of Donnie and Teddy,* in which two kids fight and insult each other. They battle it out in a sandbox, at a playground, by a lake, and at a birthday party, and in the end, a parent or teacher steps in to break up the fight and tell them they have been bad, bad boys.

Next I had an idea for a cartoon book, and as by magic, an artist I had worked with 20 years before suddenly contacted me about pitching a book of his to publishers. He had the perfect cartoon style for the project, and we created a series of books with illustrations of Trump as a nut (*Trump Is Nuts!*), as different extinct beasts (*Trump Is Extinct...Or Maybe Soon*), and as various male animals fighting for power, territory, or mates (*Trump Is an Animal!*).

Then, as Trump battled with Comey over the FBI investigation, made threats to North Korea, and fought with the media and many others in politics and entertainment, I wrote a series of poems illustrated with the many cartoons and photos posted freely around the web -- *An Ode to Donald Trump: Donald Trump, You're a Joke!; Dear Donald Trump, What's Wrong with the FBI?;* and *Dear Donald Trump, Are We Going to War?*

I thought that would be the last of the books, but as Trump began attacking all sorts of people -- including Mexicans, Muslims, a disabled reporter, and TV journalists, I was inspired to write still more columns for the *Huffington Post,* which later were combined into a book. A few of these columns addressed the question of whether Trump was nuts or had early stage Alzheimer's, citing comments from psychiatrists and psychologists, as well as my own research on lying that led to several books: *The Truth About Lying* and *Lies and Liars: How and Why Sociopaths Lie and How You Can Detect and Deal with Them.* The last of these columns ended with my thoughts on how the naked Trump statues in five U.S. cities showed his true nature.

But a few months after all this, Trump won anyway, and this has been a very tumultuous year to say the least. Now, as of this writing, after the Republican losses in elections in traditionally Republican states -- and most recently Moore's defeat in Alabama, the tide seems to be turning. Numerous White House staffers and advisers have resigned, and many news accounts suggest that the White House is in a state of constant turmoil and chaos. Also, more and more reports of Trump's erratic behavior are coming out, and the fighting against a growing number of opponents has continued. -- most recently with attacks of women accusing him of harassment at a time when many once powerful men are being discredited for their misbehavior with women. Meanwhile, the threat of war has been heating up with Trump's continued insults of Kim Jong Un of North Korea.

So these books written during the election campaign and the first months of Trump's presidency through April 2017 have proved very predictive about the way things are now.

In that spirit, I have combined all of them together into this single book I call *The Donald Trump Papers.* For the most part, these writings reflect a dark humor, although some of the commentaries and the underlying warnings in these fairy tales, myths, cartoons, adult books for kids, and poems are very serious -- yes, very serious indeed!

The sections of the book are organized in the order in which I wrote each of these books about Trump.

PART I: FAIRY TALES AND MYTHS

2016 ELECTION FAIRY TALES

9 Fairy Tales That Explain the 2016 Election Campaign

INTRODUCTION

2016 ELECTION FAIRY TALES was inspired by watching this crazy election unfold, as the conflict turned into a circus and prize fight. Instead of the usual debate about issues and opinions, the campaign became an arena of high drama, especially for Republicans, as Donald Trump, once considered just a reality show entertainer, captured the anti-establishment vote and became the front runner. Along the way, he insulted large swaths of people from woman and Mexicans to Muslims, the media, and other candidates, and he combined misstatements and lies with vulgar language and jokes. But the more outrageous his remarks, the more he got more supporters, and soon the other candidates responded in kind. Meanwhile, Hillary Clinton battled it out with Bernie Sanders, and they escalated their attacks on each other.

This growing conflict led me to think of the way traditional fairy tales can help to explain what's going on and suggest possible outcomes, since these tales recount in a simple way the battle between good and evil from the perspective of the less powerful who are up against the more powerful. Then, they commonly manage to outwit the villains and win, though the outcome of this election is still unknown. It's in that spirit that I wrote these fairy tales describing what's going on in the election today. The 9 fairy tales include:
- Two Fairy Tales about Donald Trump
- Snow White and the Seven Candidates
- Little Red Riding Hood and the Big Bad Trump
- The Three Little Pigs and the Big Bad Trump
- Golditrump and the Three Bears
- Hansel and Gretel and the Gingertrump House
- Chicken Little and the Boy Who Cried Trump

CHAPTER 1: TWO FAIRY TALES ABOUT DONALD TRUMP

    I've been reading the recent horror stories about Donald Trump from the media, establishment Republicans, writers and others, and I wondered what more I can add to the conversation. It seems like no matter who Donald Trump insults, no matter who he aligns with, no matter what he says, even if provably untrue, a large percentage of mostly less educated and lower income individuals flock to his banner. Hasn't it all been said?

    Then I realized, no it hasn't. There are two fairy tales that are very instructive, and as a sociologist and children's book writer, I think they help us understand about what is going on. And just as fairy tales have long provided an important moral message from the perspective of the less powerful lower income groups who feel exploited by the rich and powerful, these two fairy tales help to show what happens today.

    One is *The Emperor's New Clothes* by Hans Christian Anderson, published in 1837 in Denmark. The story tells the tale of an Emperor who was very fond of new clothes, so he spent all his money on them. One day, two weavers came to town and said they could weave cloth of the most beautiful colors and patterns, but these clothes would be invisible to everyone who was unfit for the job he held or was stupid or incompetent. So the Emperor paid large sums of money to both weavers to know what men in his kingdom were unfit for their jobs or foolish. But the weavers really created nothing at all as they pretended to weave at their looms. Even so, neither the Emperor nor his courtiers were willing to say they saw nothing, and when the weavers pretended to put on his new suit, telling the Emperor how wonderful he looked, he went out wearing nothing at all. He wanted to show his people how great he appeared, while his courtiers pretended to carry his long train – because, of course, no one wanted to appear foolish. Then, as the Emperor paraded around before his subjects in his "new" clothes, no one dared to say that they didn't see him wearing anything. But suddenly, a little child cried out: "But the Emperor has nothing at all on." At that, what the child said was whispered from one person to another, and everyone finally was ready to say the truth – that the Emperor had no clothes.

In turn, I think all of Trump's claims are much like that – and no matter what anyone says to call him on his exaggerations, insults, and lies, no one seems to care. So where is that little child now that we need him or her?

The other tale that I think is especially relevant today is the story of the Pied Piper of Hamelin, which comes from the town of Hamelin in Lower Saxony, Germany from the Middle Ages. The tale has been told many times, including by the Brothers Grimm. As the story goes, while the town was suffering from a rat infestation, a piper dressed in bright red clothing appeared claiming to be a rat catcher. He promised the mayor he would remove the rats, and the mayor promised to pay him. So the piper played his pipe to lure the rats into the river, where all but one drowned. But the mayor refused to pay him the full amount. So the piper vowed to return to take revenge, and one a day when the townspeople were all in church, he dressed in green like a hunter and played his pipe. He attracted the town's children, who followed him out of town into a cave and were never seen again. Or in some versions of the tale, the children followed him into the river and all drowned.

For me, Trump's followers are a little like these children who hear the pipes playing and follow blindly, mesmerized by the sound of the music because the piper plays so well. So where is the townsperson that will take away the piper's pipes so no one will follow? And where is the person who can pay off the piper what he is due, so he will take his pipes and go away?

To me these children's stories help present in a very simple way the problem we are facing today. People don't seem to want to admit that the Emperor has no clothes, so they just follow the Emperor blindly, even though he may be leading them off a cliff into a river to drown. I think it's time that we all wake up and look beneath the entertainment to the real message, whether it's by Donald Trump or Donald Drumpf. It's time to wake up America, before it's too late!

CHAPTER 2: SNOW WHITE AND THE SEVEN CANDIDATES

The 2016 campaign is becoming more and more rancorous each day, and the next two weeks after super-Tuesday promises another battle royale until the possible crowning of the king or queen of each party on Super-Duper Tuesday on March 15. Now I have been thinking of the whole campaign as something of a fairy tale, with a princess in trouble and a battle of evil between good with a goal of defeating evil at the end.

So if this is like a fairy tale, which one? The story of Snow White and the Seven Dwarfs immediately comes to mind, although in this case, I would call it Snow White and the Seven Candidates, who are trying to put Snow White away. In the original story, the seven dwarfs are trying to protect her after she falls asleep from eating a poisonous apple, so the evil step-mother queen can't kill her. But in the quest for the White House fairy tale, the seven candidates are in a heated battle to be the knight to dispatch her.

In case anyone has been asleep themselves, the Snow White story comes from a 1937 Walt Disney musical fantasy film *Snow White and the Seven Dwarfs*, which was itself adapted from the tale of Snow White by the Grimm Brothers published back in 1812, and before then was a popular folktale known throughout Europe. In brief, Snow White's step-mother keeps looking in the mirror and asking herself, "Who is the fairest in the land?" as Snow White grows up, and is reassured she is, until the mirror tells her the most beautiful woman is now Snow White, so the step-mother seeks to kill her. When Snow White flees into the forest, she hides in a cottage belonging to seven dwarfs who work in the mines for jewels, and they agree to protect her if she will keep the place clean for them. But eventually, the evil queen goes to the cottage and tricks Snow White into eating a poisoned apple, so Snow White falls asleep. Afterwards, the dwarfs and woodland creatures take care of her, until a prince kisses her, which breaks the spell and awakens her, whereupon the prince takes her to his castle. Meanwhile the evil queen meets her just deserts upon leaving the cottage, when the dwarves and animals chase her and she falls off a cliff to her death.

    Well, if the 2016 campaign is like the Snow White fairy tale, who are Snow White and the Seven Dwarfs …er…Candidates? Obviously, Hillary Clinton is Snow White, and the evil witch might be akin to the Republican Party, which is trying to get rid of her and the Democratic Party, so it can be chosen by the voters as the fairest in the land.

    Meanwhile, the seven Candidates, rather than trying to help and protect Snow White from the devious machinations of the evil queen, they are first trying to fight and outwit each other before they take her on. So who are they? Well, there's Doc, aka Donald Trump, who might be considered the leader of the pack, at least for now, though they are all ganging up on him. Then, there's Grumpy, AKA Bernie Sanders, who is complaining about all the things wrong with America and what to do to fix it, but most Americans doubt he can really do that, so for now the other dwarfs are mostly ignoring him. Another popular dwarf is Sleepy, AKA Ben Carson, who doesn't do much except sleepily give some odd answers about how he's going to wake up the people, but then he drifts off back to sleep – and most recently, he decided he would rather sleep off the campaign train.

Other dwarfs include Dopey, AKA Chris Christie, who dopily tried to take down one of the other dwarfs by claiming he was just a robot and dropped out of the campaign himself. Then, he tried to find favor with the leader of the campaign, which was really a dopey move, since he lost favor with his own supporters, many of whom stopped supporting him, while others have claimed his political career is ruined.

Still another dwarf is Happy, AKA Marco Rubio, though he isn't very happy anymore. For a while, he tried to put a happy face on everything he was doing, even when he was losing, and he kept trying to keep the party going strong, even as all the balloons were losing their air. Then, he tried changing his name to Angry, but that didn't work too well. So now maybe he might be called Dazed or Confused, while he hopes the party will want him to stay on and he tries to revive it. But if he can't, well, maybe he'll just become Lost or what Doc calls a Loser. And that's too bad, because it was nice to see him as Happy.

Then, too, there is Sneezy, AKA Ted Cruz, who is always sneezing up a storm because he has all sorts of allergies, and he can blow away anything or anyone in his path. That's why the other dwarfs usually hold their nose when he's around, which sounds about right. As a candidate, he doesn't like many other people very much and wants to ship millions of people back home, and the other people in his group don't like him very much either.

Finally, last but not least there's Bashful (aka John Kasich), who is quietly trying to present himself as the one adult, who can help to take over party leadership from Doc before it's too late. Then, he can victoriously lead the charge against Snow White and put her away for good. But more and more it looks like it's too late for him, because who wants a Bashful fighter, when it's more fun and entertaining to see a team of fighters fighting among themselves to see who will win the right to take on Snow White and win it all for the Evil Queen – AKA the Republican Party.

But then, as it goes in the original folktale and Disney Story, the Evil Queen falls to her death over a cliff, which is seems to be what is happening to the Republican Party now.

CHAPTER 3: LITTLE RED RIDING HOOD AND THE BIG BAD TRUMP

As the 2016 campaign has been heating up and the insults are flying fast and furiously, I've been seeing it more and more like the traditional fairy tales, where an underdog battles the forces of evil and ultimately prevails. In this case the victory would be winning the race and being crowned king or queen – whoops, President – for the next four years. And usually the villain is an evil king or queen, or some much feared dangerous predator, such as a wily wolf.

Now what seems like an especially fitting way to describe the events of the last few days is the story of Little Red Riding Hood and the Big Bad Wolf – now called the Big Bad Trump. As is well known, the basic story is that an innocent girl walking through the woods is tricked by the evil wolf to tell him where she is going. Then, he jumps into her bed and poses as her grandmother, so he can eat her, but she escapes, and goodbye, big bad wolf. Some commenters on the story have seen the underlying message as an attempt at sexual seduction, where a potential victim escapes. But putting that idea aside, this seems like a great parable for what is happening in today's political campaign.

In this case, the original story comes from a European fairy tale dating back to the 10th century, where it was told by French peasants and later by Italian peasants. Eventually, it was published in 1697 by Charles Perrault and later by the Grimm Brothers in 1812. Some of this additional detail is especially relevant for the modern-day political drama.

In brief, once upon a time there was a little girl, who was loved by everyone, especially by her grandmother, who gave her a little red riding hood, which led her to be called Little Red Riding Hood. Today, perhaps think of grandma being like the Democratic Party giving Hillary Clinton her mantle to run. Then, one day, Little Red's mother gave her some cake and a bottle of wine to take to her ill grandmother, so she would feel better, much like the DNC chair gave Hillary lots of money to help the party recover its mojo and obtain victory.

But, as the story goes, Little Red met the wolf along the way, who enticed her to tell him where she was going, since he was eager to eat up both Little Red and her grandmother, just as one time, Donald Trump gave money to the Democratic Party and hosted Hillary and husband Bill at his 2005 wedding to Melania Knauss, his third wife, at Mar-a-Lago in Palm Beach. So just like the wolf seemed to be a great friend as he accompanied Little Red through the woods and invited her to listen to the birds and pick flowers, while he ran to her grandmother's house, Trump seemed to be a great supporter of the Clinton's – that is, until he decided to run against her.

Think of his decision to run against her as a little like the wolf devouring Little Red's grandmother and getting in her bed, pretending to be grandma, with her cap pulled down over his face. Then, when Little Red notices that her grandmother looks very strange, asking "What a deep voice you have…what big ears you have…what big eye you have…" concluding with "what big hands you have" and "what a big mouth you have," the wolf always has a ready answer just like Trump. No matter the question, the wolf or Trump has an answer, which ends with the final answer: "All the better to eat you with!" After that the wolf/Trump pounces and eats her up. So you might think the wolf has finally won.

But then along comes a passing huntsman, who hears the wolf, who has just fallen asleep and is snoring after his tasty meal. So the hunter goes to check on grandma, sees the wolf in bed, cuts open his stomach, and out pops Little Red and grandma. Then, they all fetch big stones, fill up the wolf's belly, and when he gets up and tries to run away, the stones are so heavy that he falls down dead. Afterwards, the huntsman goes home with the wolf's skin as a trophy, the grandmother eats the cake and the wine, and Little Red goes home determined to never leave the path by herself.

The ending of the story is the perfect parable to what may happen today. So who's the huntsman? Well, it could be any of the Republicans who are going after Trump, so they can get rid of him – from Rubio, Cruz, and Kasich to

Romney and the big Establishment donors. After they are finished carving up the Big Bad Trump so his campaign collapses, they can at least feel happy they have succeeded in taking down their big game trophy. At the same time, they have left the path clear, so the DNC can now enjoy the fruits of success, as Little Red goes back on the path to victory, now that the Big Bad Trump is gone. And the other Republicans who have hunted Trump down have gone away, too – this time because they are so weakened by fighting each other that they need more time to get their next hunting party together for a future hunt.

CHAPTER 4: THE THREE LITTLE PIGS AND THE BIG BAD TRUMP

Here's another 2016 campaign fairy tale inspired by all the attacks, insults, name-calling, jokes, and down in the gutter humor. Some of these tales capture perfectly the anger and frustration of the voters watching a spectacle that becomes wilder and crazier each day. In this case, the political pigs who are subjected to the taunts and threats of a dangerous beast struggle to stay alive, and one finally finds a way to end the threat – just as Marco Rubio, Ted Cruz, and Hillary Clinton are battling Donald Trump for their political survival.

The Story of the Three Little Pigs and the Big Bad Wolf" is another tale that is a perfect fit with what's happening in the election campaign. Rubio builds his house of straw, but it is easily blown down by the Big Bad Trump. Cruz builds his house of sticks, which is a little stronger, but the Big Bad Trump blows a little harder and knocks it down. Finally, Hillary creates an even stronger house of bricks, which is like her wall of security personnel, press people, assistants, and others she surrounds herself with for protection. Thus, she is able to stand up to the Big Bad Trump, so he not only can't blow her house down, but he gets all burned up in the process. That's just like what happens in the traditional story, where the wolf gets outwitted, and in the end, the little pig with the brick home is the last pig standing, because the bricks are stronger, and the pig is more crafty in getting the wolf to fall for some sneaky tricks. In the story – as in politics.

In this case, the original story, which comes from British folklore, was first printed in the 1840s. Then, it was included as "The Three Little Pigs" in *The Nursery Rhymes of England*, published in 1886, and it was republished in its best known form in 1890 in *English Fairy Tales*. In the traditional tale, the pig's mother doesn't have enough to support the family, so she sends the three pigs out to seek their fortune – you might think of the Republican and Democratic Parties sending out their chosen candidates to make their way in campaigning for the election.

Along the way, the three pigs (aka candidates – Marco Rubio, Ted Cruz, and Hillary Clinton) – encounter three men on the road and get the materials they need to build their houses. You might consider them like today's campaign financiers and managers. The first little pig, Rubio, gets a bundle of straw and builds his house with that. The second little pig, Cruz, gets a bundle of sticks for his house. And the third little pig, Clinton, gets a load of bricks to build her house.

Then, enter the Big Bad Wolf, Trump, along the road. As the story goes, the wolf asks the first pig with the straw house to let him in, but the pig says no, so he says, "I'll huff, and I'll puff, and I'll blow your house in," and he does so. After that, in some versions of the story, the wolf eats the little pig or he escapes.

In any case, the Big Bad Trump has been doing a pretty good job of destroying Rubio's house of straw in virtually every state.

Next, as the story continues, the wolf asks the pig with the house of sticks for entry, but this pig says no, too, and the sticks, though stronger than straw, are not strong enough. So the wolf takes down this house, after which he eats up this pig or he escapes, much like the Big Bad Trump has been knocking down Cruz in most states.

But at the third house of bricks, the house is too strong. So though the wolf huffs and puffs again and again, he can't blow the house down. Then, he tries to trick the pig to come out of the house by asking to meet in various places. But the pig is too smart and outwits him each time, much like Clinton has managed to evade Trump's assorted attacks on her record and is still prevailing even more strongly in the Democratic race.

Finally, the wolf decides to sneak into the chimney and get the little pig that way. But the pig is too smart for him, puts a pot of water on a blazing fire, and just as the wolf comes down, the pig takes off the cover, and the wolf falls in. After that the little pig eats the wolf for supper and lives happily ever after, though in another version the wolf runs away with a burned rump and never goes back. In either case, the little pig with the brick house survives and thrives, much like what might happen in a Hillary Clinton and Donald Trump match-up, and Clinton outsmarts Trump. If so, as the story might end, she might either eat him up in the election tallies or he might run off back to his Trump businesses, and she and the country might live happily ever after. If only real life was like that.

CHAPTER 5: GOLDITRUMP AND THE THREE BEARS

After seeing the latest 2016 campaign debates that were filled with even more attacks, insults, and down and dirty humor, I thought of a traditional fairy tale that highlights the frustration of those who feel put upon and exploited by those who are more powerful. In this case, they just hope the offending person will just go away, so they can get their house back in order – in this case the Republican house.

Now with the three remaining Republican candidates joining together to get rid of Trump, what would be more fitting than the story of Goldilocks and the Three Bears, where Trump is Goldilocks with his blonde hair, while Rubio, Cruz, and Kasich are the remaining three bears. In the traditional story, the three bears – mama, papa, and baby bear – come home to see their cottage has been ransacked, and they discover the intruder, Goldilocks, sleeping in their bed, whereupon Goldilocks flees, and the bears are happy they have their home back. Which seems to be exactly what the three remaining candidates want. Goodbye Trump. Just go away. Then, the three candidates and the Republican Party are happy again.

In this case, the original story, which was part of British folklore, was first published in 1837 by Robert Southey, a British writer and poet. He called it "The Story of the Three Bears," and it was about a little bear, middle-sized bear, and huge bear, who live in a house in the woods, and they each have their own porridge bowl, chair, and bed. Significantly, while they are out for a walk in the woods, an intruder who enters their house is an old ugly woman, who is considered impudent, bad, foul-mouthed, and deserving of a stint in the House of Corrections, which sounds like some of the accusations leveled at Trump. But eventually, the old woman was turned into a pretty little girl in 1849, when Joseph Cundall published his *Treasury of Pleasure Books for Young Children*, and after twenty more years the girl became known as Golden Hair and finally Goldilocks in *Old Nursery Stories and Rhymes,* published in 1904.

But however you slice and dice it, this description of the old foul-mouth intruder or girl with the golden hair seems to perfectly fit Trump based on his behavior and yellow mop of hair.

The story seems a perfect fit, too. As the popular story of Goldilocks goes, after she knocks upon the house in the forest, which might be compared to the Republican Party, she finds no one home. She knocks and when no one answers, she walks right in – just like Trump did when he announced his candidacy. Then, she sees three bowls of porridge on the table, finds the first one too hot, the second one too cold, and the third one just right, which might be like Trump deciding on his strategy, as he first insults some Mexican immigrants as rapists, insults Megyn Kelly and other women, and finds that his attacks on Muslims and deporting illegal immigrants are just about right.

Then, as the story continues, after Goldilocks eats up the three bears' breakfasts, she walks into the living room and sees three chairs. She finds the first and second ones too big, but when she sits down in the smallest chair, it breaks into pieces – just like what seems to be happening to the Republican party.

After that, feeling very tired, Goldilocks lays down to rest, but she finds the first bed too hard, perhaps like Ted Cruz; the second bed too soft, perhaps like Marco Rubio; and then she lies down in the third bed and finds it very comfortable. Perhaps think of John Kasich, trying to be the adult of the remaining candidates. Then, she falls asleep.

That's when the bears come back. You might consider the big bear like Ted Cruz, who's full of anger and bluster; the little bear, like Marco Rubio, sometimes called "Little Rubio" by Trump; and the medium sized bear, as John Kaisich, since he's tried to navigate a middle course and stay calm, while all around him is uproar and fury.

In any case, after the three bears confront Goldilocks together, she screams "Help," jumps up, runs out the door back into the forest, and never comes back to the home of the three bears. And that would seem to be the outcome the three Republican bears would like – to have Trump leave their Republican Party home for good.

CHAPTER 6: HANSEL AND GRETEL AND THE GINGERTRUMP HOUSE

"Hansel and Gretel" is another traditional fairy tale that helps us understand what's going on in this crazy campaign that has drawn in anti-establishment voters who are angry, since they have been beaten down by the economy and want changes to the way things are. The story of Hansel and Gretel helps to illustrate the saga of these voters, since they are lost in the woods, seek refuge in what looks like an attractive place to go, and are threatened by destruction by an evil witch who has lured them in, only to try to eat them up before they manage to escape.

In this case, the original story, which comes from German folklore, was first recorded and published by the Brothers Grimm in 1812. As the story goes, Hansel and Gretel are young children whose father is a woodcutter, and when a great famine occurs, his abusive second wife convinces him to send the kids into the woods, because they eat too much, so she and her husband won't starve to death. The situation is a little like today's economic turmoil that's resulting in increased inequality, so many once middle-class people and poor people are suffering more and more, and so can feel very lost. Thus, as you think of Hansel and Gretel going off into the woods, you might think of the Republican and Democratic Party struggling to find its own way and survive.

At first, Hansel and Gretel try to return home after Hansel lays out a trail of pebbles and then breadcrumbs, but that doesn't work very well, much like it has proved difficult to get any bills through Congress to help the poor and downtrodden. But eventually Hansel and Gretel follow a beautiful white bird, who is singing so delightfully, to a house in the woods built of bread and covered with cakes and windows of clear sugar. So since the children are so tired and hungry, they start eating the roof and windows of the house. This inviting attraction is a little like the way Trump has sent out his call to the angry and frustrated people, using sweet enticing words and entertaining antics to woo them, which he knows how to do well as a reality show host featuring glamourous celebrities. So his promises and claims of greatness and success are like sweet candy to voters, so they eagerly follow and vote for him. They think it will be just great in the gingerbread house built by Trump.

But then, as the traditional story goes, a hideous old woman comes out of the house and lures Hansel and Gretel inside with the promise of good food and soft beds. As a result, after having a wonderful meal, the children lay down to sleep in beds with linen sheets, feeling like they are in heaven. But in fact, the old woman had only pretended to be kind, because she is in reality a wicked witch, who built her house of bread in order to cook and eat the children who fall into her power, just like Trump might seek to use his power if elected President to do whatever he wants, such as building a wall to keep out Mexicans, preventing Muslims from entering the country, torturing suspected terrorists, and killing their innocent family members. And the gingerbread house is, of course, like one of Trump's many real estate properties.

In any case, poor Hansel and Gretel are at first helpless. The witch locks Hansel in a cage in a stable behind a grated door to fatten him up, so she can eat him, much like Trump has been capturing the Republican Party by rounding up more votes than anyone else. He has done so by reshaping the debates, so he can insult and demean the other candidates, while they have little success in fighting back, much like Hansel in his cage. Trump just insults the opposing candidates some more and looks for their weaknesses to undermine them, such as repeatedly calling Cruz a liar and attacking Rubio as too weak and soft to make a good President. Still, Hansel is able to keep the witch from eating him by holding out a little bone, which she thinks is his finger, so she continues to think he is still too thin to eat, much like the remaining Republican candidates, Cruz, Rubio, and Kasich, keep entering primaries and caucuses in the hope of getting enough votes to stop Trump from winning the nomination.

Meanwhile, the witch treats Gretel like a slave, ordering her around to cook and fetch water, much like Trump has been putting down Hillary, as not being worthy of being President, accusing her of everything from the e-mail scandal to lying about the attacks in Benghazi and having a husband with a roving eye.

But finally, Gretel proves to be the smart one. After the witch decides to eat Hansel even if he is too thin, she prepares the oven for him and decides to kill Gretel, too. So she asks Gretel to open the oven and lean in front of it to see if the fire is hot enough. But suspecting that the witch plans to kill her, Gretel pretends she doesn't understand what the witch wants her to do. So she asks the witch to show her. Once the witch demonstrates, Gretel pushes her into the oven and shuts and bolts the iron door, after which the witch burns to death. Then, she frees Hansel, and they discover chests of pearls and jewels throughout the witch's house, which they take back home with them. Likewise, the wily Hillary can be the one to successfully attack Trump, whether he wins the nomination or not, and the witch's house with its treasures and precious stones is much like Trump's beautiful three-floor penthouse in Manhattan, which is filled with luxurious paintings and furniture, like a room from a Louis XIV palace. And in the end, the witch is burnt up, much like Trump might feel burned should he lose the nomination to Cruz, Rubio, or other establishment Republican, or should he lose badly to Hillary in the election in November. In that case, no wonder Trump might feel all burned up, because he has lost despite all his insults, lies, and low-blow attacks, much like the evil witch ended up getting destroyed in her own oven.

CHAPTER 7: CHICKEN LITTLE AND THE BOY WHO CRIED TRUMP

I thought these last two fairy tales might be a fitting end to this crazy election campaign, in which many think the U.S. voters have lost their political minds to an entertaining spectacle that is more like a prize fight than a fight for the Presidential prize. One is the story of Chicken Little, who thinks the end of the world is nigh after an acorn falls on her head, and she gets others to race with her to tell the king, only to be captured and eaten by a fox. The other story is about a shepherd boy who cries wolf several times just for fun. But no one believes him when a real wolf appears, so the wolf eats his sheep.

The Chicken Little story, sometimes called "Henny Penny," comes originally from the oral folk tradition in Europe, where it was told in Germany and Denmark in the 19th century. Then, it was published by the Brothers Grimm and later published in English in Scotland in 1842 by Robert Chambers in *Popular Rhymes, Fireside Stories, and Amusements of Scotland,* which became the basis for various versions that appeared after that.

In the basic story, a chick called Chicken Little, believes the sky is falling, when an acorn falls on her head. So she runs to tell the king, and along the way meets a number of other barnyard fowl, which include Henny Penny, Ducky Lucky, Goosey Loosey, and Turkey Lurkey. They agree it is terrible that the sky is falling, and they run along with Chicken Little, without bothering to check out what Chicken Little has told them. Their race is like the many Republican Party establishment candidates running to save America from the terrible fate of Hillary Clinton or Donald Trump. So who's who? Well, maybe they might be Jeb Bush or Ben Carson as Chicken Little, Carly Fiorina as Henny Penny, Marco Rubio as Ducky Lucky, Chris Christie or John Kasich as Goosey Loosey, and Ted Cruz as Turkey Lurkey. Or shift the names around, since they all think they are running for their lives because the sky is falling, though they just take Chicken Little's word for it.

Then they meet Foxy Loxy, who is crafty like Donald Trump, and he asks the question: "How do you know the sky is falling?" When Chicken Little claims she saw and heard it and felt a piece of the sky fall on her head, Foxy Loxy invites everyone to follow him and he'll show them the way to the king. But instead, he takes them to his lair and eats them all – which seems to be what's happening to all the other Republican candidates and to the Republican party itself. Trump is leading them along in the glare of the media, saying whatever he wants, and getting other candidates to stoop to his own level, whereupon they self-destruct, because no one can beat Foxy Loxy at his own game.

As for the Boy Who Cried Wolf, that's one of Aesop's fables, which dates from classical times in Greece and was translated into Latin in the 15th century, after which it was translated into other languages and spread through Europe. It finally was published in English in 1867 by George Fyler Townsend as "The Shepherd and the Wolf." As a political fairy tale, it might be called "The Boy Who Cried Trump." In the traditional story, a shepherd boy gets bored watching the village sheep and to amuse himself, he calls out: "Wolf! Wolf! The Wolf is chasing the sheep!" In response, the villagers come running up the hill to help the boy but find no wolf. Then, he calls out "Wolf! Wolf!" again, and once more the villagers come running but see no wolf. As a result, when the boy sees a real wolf and calls out "Wolf! Wolf!" the villagers ignore him, and the wolf eats his sheep. And in some versions of the tale, the wolf eats the boy.

Well, in this case, the boy crying wolf the first time is a little like the Republican Party and the media thinking Trump running for President is just a joke or publicity stunt to build his own brand, so they ignore any calls in the beginning to take him seriously. So Trump gets lots of press when he makes outrageous statements, like putting down Megyn Kelly, calling some Mexicans coming to the U.S. rapists, and issuing a call to ban Muslims. In fact, some media categorize his campaign as entertainment and all in fun. Meanwhile, Trump is gathering more and more support, until it's too late, and he is able to swoop in like the wolf, because everyone ignores the early warnings, believing they aren't true.

Thus, now, even if the sky is really falling, it could be too late to do anything about it. Trump, much like the fox and wolf, has eaten up the competition, and now he can eat up the sheep and anyone else who gets in his way.

THE VERY GREAT MONSTER IN THE WHITE HOUSE
(AKA: 2016 ELECTION MONSTER MYTHS)

15 Monster Myths That Explain
the Battle Against Donald Trump

CHAPTER 1: TRUMP AND THE MONSTER MYTH MASH

I recently wrote a series of fairy tales inspired by this crazy election, such as Chicken Little and the Boy Who Cried Trump and The Three Little Pigs and the Big Bad Trump, which were published as *9 Election Fairy Tales: 9 Fair Tales that Explain the 2016 Election Campaign*. Now after seeing the increasing violence at Trump rallies, spurred on by his rhetoric filled with insults, put-downs, racist remarks, taunts, and suggestions about attacking others, I thought about how every society has had its scary monsters and he was like one of these monsters. In fact, many people have compared Trump to Hitler and the loyalty pledge to him like a Nazi salute. And videos have shown how Trump has egged on the fights on by pointing at people who have disagreed with something he said or might look disruptive. Then, his security forces have grabbed them and carried them out, such as at one rally in Fayette, North Carolina, where one woman said the man they were taking away had done nothing, and then they dragged her out, too.

Those photos and videos of chaos and confrontations along with supportive cheers at his rallies have led me to look at this long tradition of powerful and dangerous monsters, where many people become victims, though sometimes, a hero emerges who is able to confront and defeat the monster in battle. In American popular culture, we have tamed many of these monsters in our films and media, so they have become an image of fun, such as in the Disney films *Monsters University* and the *Shrek* series. And even before then there was the popular 1962 *Monster Mash* song by Bobby Picket, in which a mad scientist's monster emerges from the slab to perform a dance that becomes the hit of the land when other monsters, including Dracula, come to the party. But historically, in other cultures, these monsters are truly scary.

In many ways, so is Donald Trump very scary today, especially to most other Republicans, to Democrats, and to much of the media, Hollywood stars, academics, minority group members, women, and others he has insulted or belittled on his way to the top. While some fervently support him and cheer like fans at a boxing match, he has polarized the country along the way.

Thus, since Trump has become to many the essence of a monster who threatens to not only destroy the Republican Party, but the country as a whole, I thought it fitting to see how Trump might compare to other monsters through traditional myth and legend. In some cases, the monster seems to prevail and the people are urged to stay away or get killed, while at times, a hero emerges to slay the monster, like St. George who slays the dragon. This story of St. George and the Dragon dates back to the 7th century and the Eastern Orthodox Church. It was brought back to Western Europe by the Crusaders in the 10th or 11th century. Then, it was written up in Jacobus de Voragine's *Golden Legend* in about 1260 and the dragon's lair was set in Libya. Over the next centuries, it gradually it became a part of the Christian tradition.

As the story goes, a town had a small lake with a plague-bearing dragon who was poisoning the countryside. To appease it, the people fed it two sheep every day, and when they ran out of sheep, they began feeding it their children, chosen by lottery. Then, one day the king's daughter was chosen, and the grieving king told the people they could have all his gold and silver and half his kingdom if his daughter was spared. But after the people refused, he sent his daughter to the lake, dressed as a bride to be fed to the dragon. But before the dragon could eat her, Saint George rode by the lake, wounded the dragon, and led it and the princess back to the city, where the dragon terrified everyone. Saint George offered to kill the dragon if the people agreed to be Christians and be baptized, after which 15,000 people and the king converted, and George killed the dragon. In other versions of the story, St. George goes to save the princess from being sacrificed, and after the dragon rushes from its cave, St. George kills the dragon with his sword by piercing it under its wing where there are no scales.

Well, in this case, Trump might be compared to the dragon, and much of America to the people of the town who are terrorized by the dragon. As for the princess St. George goes to save, that might be the spirit of liberty and freedom that might be destroyed if the Trump dragon gobbles her up, because he wants everyone to be loyal to him and do exactly what he wants. If not, he will insult and destroy them, such as by killing the families of suspected terrorists, deporting 11 million undocumented immigrants, and arresting anyone who dares to protest.

As the traditional story describes, this dragon poisoned and ravaged the countryside with its venomous breath, roared with a sound louder than thunder, and had an immense head and tail fifty feet long. Plus his very hard scales were hard to penetrate, until St. George found a soft spot under its wing. Fast forward to today, and the dragon's venomous breath might be compared to Trump's poisonous insulting words, while its loud roars might be compared to Trump's use of the bully pulpit at his raucous rallies, his TV appearances, and regular tweets. And the dragon's immense head and tail might be compared to Trump's hair and ummm…well, his recent claims about that in response to Rubio's taunts. Finally, the dragon's scales might be compared to Trump's ability to fend off any criticisms or attacks on himself with damaging attacks on his opponents.

In the story, St. George is able to find a vulnerable spot. So what about today? Well, it's not clear what that spot is or who will find it. But as they say, the pen is mightier than the sword. So maybe all the recent stories about Trump's bankruptcies, the Trump University lawsuits, his hiring workers from Poland and China, his many misstatements and lies, or other investigative pieces may be what brings Trump down. Or maybe Trump will start to open up himself to criticism himself, such as when he shows off Trump Steaks and Wine, like he is making a commercial for his product line, rather than running for President and finding ways to help the people. And so the world awaits a modern day St. George who might bring down the dangerous dragon.

CHAPTER 2: IS TRUMP A CHIMERA?

Can Trump and the circus of a political campaign surrounding him be described as a chimera? Today the word "chimera" refers to a creation of the imagination or an impossible and foolish fancy, while someone or something that is "chimerical" is given to unrealistic fantasies. But the words come from the Chimera monster in Greek mythology, which has the body and head of a lion with a snake for its tail and a fire-breathing goat head coming from its back. In some versions of the myth, the creature has wings on its back. The word is also used in scientific research to explain an animal with more than one set of genetic codings, since the Greek monster is a combination of three different normal animals.

Now after I have been following the latest uproar from the violence at Trump's rallies, it would seem that this description fits Trump to a T for Trump. For example, there has always been something fantastic about Trump's campaign, which some believed he started as a kind of entertainment to build his brand. As a result, for several months, other politicians and the media didn't take him seriously, so he got all kinds of free press coverage, as if he was involved in a political reality show. But in a "show" with one final winner, after others are booted off the island – akin to ending their political campaign, Trump is really in it to win. Or maybe the campaign started off as a political lark; then as Trump started attracting supporters at his rallies, he began to take it seriously. In either case, part of Trump's appeal is his promise that he will "Make America Great Again," but so many of his proposals may turn out to be very unrealistic, such as his plan to deport 11 million illegal immigrants or his plan to build a wall between the U.S. and Mexico and get Mexico to pay for it. Numerous political scientists, pundits, and economists have already pointed out how his plans won't work in reality. But people still seem to follow him because they want to believe.

As for the Chimera having the head of a lion, a tail of a snake, and a fire-breathing goat, one can imagine that Trump has those qualities. For one thing, he is all about power and control, and he has the fury of the lion, too, such as when he directs his security personnel to eject anyone from his rallies who dares to confront him with unfriendly questions or anti-Trump posters or T-shirts. His remarks that people might deserve to be roughed up and his call to bring back waterboarding and other forms of torture for enemies are another example of how the lion might treat his hapless victim, who gets torn apart by his massive teeth and jaws.

As for the snake, that's a perfect comparison, too, since snakes are crafty and wily. They slither through the grass, hidden away, until ready to strike, and the term "snake" is often used today to refer to someone who lies. And that's what Trump does. Again and again, he has misstated facts and later claimed he didn't misstate them. He has said he would do one thing, but has then done another. He has made promises and then denied them, such as recently stating he would pay the legal bills for anyone at his rallies who roughed up a protester, but later he denied he said it. In fact, numerous videos on the Internet illustrate the discrepancies between what Trump said one time and what he said at another. So definitely, the snake fits.

Finally, the fire-breathing goat might be a fit analogy because this fire might help to burn anyone who gets in the way of the lion, much as Trump has burned through numerous other candidates, like a fire brigade setting fires to get rid of excess foliage to create a clear area. Likewise, one by one, other candidates have withered away, unable to stand up to Trump's raging attacks on them, much like a schoolyard bully can beat down any other children with their insults and physical attacks.

So what is one to do when confronting such a beast? Well, the Greek myth might provide an answer. According to this story, the Chimera came from a family of other monster gods, Typhon and Echidna, so its siblings included other famous monsters such as The Sphinx and Cerberus, the multi-headed dog who guarded Hades, the underworld. Likewise, Trump has drawn around him a family that comes to his support on the campaign trail, as well as an army of security guards to protect him. Traditionally, even seeing the Chimera was a bad omen, since he regularly appeared before disasters such as shipwrecks, violent storms, and volcanic eruptions, which might be comparable to Trump's rage at other countries, such as China, which is now experiencing a serious economic upheaval.

Yet, in the end, a Greek hero is finally able to defeat this fearsome monster. This happens when Bellerophon, riding on his trusty winged steed, Pegasus, flies by and kills the Chimera with his bow and arrow. So the Chimera is at last defeated, and the people rejoice. Now who is the modern hero who can do this? Some possibilities include John Kasich, after his win against the Trump Chimera in Ohio; Ted Cruz, who is approaching Trump in votes; or even Hillary or Bernie

Sanders in the event the Trump Chimera is able to overpower and devour still other heroes who take him on. But ultimately, as the Chimera myth goes, a hero will prevail by shooting an arrow from the sky – which today might take the form a sharp argument, revelation, or vote at a brokered Republican convention -- to take the Chimera Trump down.

CHAPTER 3: BEHEADING THE TRUMP CAMPAIGN

Today the effort to stop Trump by Republican candidates and the Party and by Democrats might be like the effort to get rid of the Medusa in Greek mythology. Medusa, for those who don't recall their Greek myths from high school, is one of the evil Gorgon sisters, and she was so fearsome, that she could turn all who came into her presence into stone. Then, along came Perseus, who cut off her head, and from her blood came the birth of Pegasus, the winged horse, which Bellerophon rode on when he shot an arrow to killed the Chimera, another monster comparable to Trump. For Trump can be compared to many different monsters, because he changes himself and his positions, like a chameleon who changes to match its colors to the environment. I've described two such comparisons in the two previous chapters "Trump and the Monster Myth Mash" and "Is Trump a Chimera?"

In any case, this is another myth about monsters that seems like a perfect fit with Trump. As the story of Medusa goes, Medusa, along with her sisters, lived in a faraway place towards the night, and Medusa was an especially formidable foe, since her hideous appearance turned any onlooker into stone. In some versions of the myth, she was born a monster like her sisters, and as such, she was encircled by serpents with vibrating tongues and huge wings, claws, and teeth. In later versions, mainly from Ovid, Medusa was the only Gorgon with snake locks, as a punishment from Athena because of Medusa's liaison with Poseidon, the god of the sea.

    A comparison of Trump with Medusa certain fits. Among other things, his life in a faraway place at night might be comparable to his jet style, lavish life in New York and his travels all over the world in his private plane. Plus, he is a formidable candidate to take on, because he quickly cracks down on whoever opposes him, whether by words or lawsuits, such as in his attacks on Megyn Kelly for standing up to him in a debate, his suit Univision when they decided not to broadcast the Miss America and Miss Universe Pageants owned by Trump, and his suit against restauranteur Jose Andres when he cancelled plans to open a restaurant in Trump's new hotel, because Trump he accused Mexicans of being rapists. Plus Trump has decimates the other Republican candidates one by one with his personal attacks and by getting legions of voters to turn away from them and vote for him. Then, too, his blonde wig might be compared to Medusa's wild snakes' locks, and perhaps his earlier flings with numerous beautiful women and two earlier marriages might be compared to Medusa's liaison with Poseidon.

    In any event, Perseus ended up confronting Medusa after Polydectes, the king, sent him on a quest to bring him her head, since Perseus didn't want the king to marry his mother, because he thought Polydectes was dishonorable. So Polydectes sought to trick Perseus by holding a large banquet to collect contributions for his marriage to Hippodamia, who tamed horses. He asked his guests to bring horses for a gift, but Perseus didn't have one and offered any gift the king wanted. That's when Polydectes asked Perseus to bring him the head of Medusa, since he wanted to disgrace and get rid of Perseus.

    However, Perseus succeeded with the aid of divine gifts, including a reflective bronze shield from Athena and a helmet of darkness which gave him invisibility from Hades. Then, with the help of the gods, he found the Gorgons' cave and killed Medusa by beheading her while she slept. After that, he put her head in a bag so no one would be turned to stone by her still strong gaze, and brought it back to the king. But along the way he used Medusa's head to turn some others who angered or opposed him to stone, too, such as Atlas, and once at the palace, he turned the king and his whole court to stone, too, and eventually he gave the head to Athena, who put it on her shield and breastplate.

    So who might be the modern day Perseus to slay the Trump Medusa or use the threat of his fearsome gaze or legion of followers to get others to join the battle against him? Well, one possibility is John Kasich, who beheaded Trump's effort to win the vote in Ohio, or Ted Cruz, who has headed off Trump's quest for votes in several other states. Or maybe Hillary might play the role of Perseus if the others can't defeat Trump. Or perhaps with some help from the Republican Party gods and their magical juggling of the votes of the delegates, that might help to slay the Trump Medusa while he sleeps, thinking all is still well.

CHAPTER 4: COULD TRUMP BE THE U.S. CYCLOPS?

As Trump has been gathering more and more voters to his fold, like a shepherd expanding his flocks, and more and more opponents attack, Trump seems much like the Cyclops encountered by Odysseus in his journey to Ithaca after the Trojan War. And since monsters in myths and legends can assume multiple forms, he might similarly be compared him to the dragon St. George fights or to a Chimera. Likewise, Trump can be compared to many other monsters, since he changes himself and his positions to suit the situation, from Trump the lamb trying to placate and unify the Republican Party to Trump the raging lion, threatening the potential for violence if the Party doesn't select him as nominee. Meanwhile, all kinds of opponents, like Odysseus, are trying to escape his wrath and defeat him.

In this case, as the story of Odysseus and the Cyclops goes, after a nine-year conflict in which the Greeks fought the city of Troy, Odysseus and his shipments were blown far off course and arrived at a large island, where shepherds tended their flocks. They found a huge goat pen outside a cave, and after finding all kinds of cheeses and meats inside, they stopped to have a feast. Later, as they were relaxing contentedly, the shepherd, Polyphemus, came home. He was one of the giant blacksmiths, called Cyclops, who had built Olympus for the gods, and he was huge, the size of a barn, with a single eye in the center of his forehead. Upon seeing the men, Polyphemus was delighted, since he could eat them up, and he promptly rolled a boulder into the mouth of the cave to keep them from leaving. Then, he snatched up two of Odysseus's men and ate them. The following day, after letting his goats out to pasture, he closed up the entrance again, and ate some more of Odysseus' men.

Immediately, some modern day parallels come to mind. You might think of all the real estate that Trump owns as like Olympus built for the gods. These properties are all sufficiently lavish and elegant that modern day wealthy gods buy them or they stay in Trump's hotels or spend the day on his golf courses playing golf. As for the flocks of goats, you might think of the mostly blue collar workers who have flocked to Trump's banner and eagerly follow him. As for the cheeses and meats, well, there are Trumps steaks, wines, and restaurants. Trump certainly keeps his eye on everything. And you might say he has eaten up most of the other candidates.

As the story continues, Odysseus creates a plan to escape. He gives the Cyclops wine, so he drifts off to sleep, whereupon Odysseus and his men fashion a pole with a point and ram it into the Cyclops' eye, blinding him, so he can't capture and eat any more of Odysseus' men. Then, when Polyphemus lets the goats out in the morning, Odysseus and his men escape by clinging to their bellies. After that, the blinded Cyclops throws another boulder at the ship, but Odysseus and his men escape and the leave Cyclops ranging impotently on the shore of the island.

Again, a modern-day comparison is apt, as the Republican Party and remaining candidates, Cruz and Kasich, plot various ways to get out of Trump's hold on his delegates, who are like Odysseus' goats. One strategy might be keeping Trump from getting enough goats…er delegates…to win the nomination, and if so, many or all of his delegates might run off, so the opponents can choose their own nominee. Meanwhile, Trump has been blindly raging at the Republican Party and hurling attacks at Cruz and Kasich, much like the blinded Cyclops impotently raged at Odysseus and his men as they sailed away on their journey. Meanwhile, still other forces have gathered to keep the blindly raging Trump Cyclops from succeeding, from the media to various ethnic groups, including many Jewish leaders and their supporters who have formed a Come Together Against Hate group to block Trump's nomination.

So will the modern day Odysseus, such as Cruz, Kasich, and the Republican Party, finally prevail in escaping from the Trump Cyclops who is raging blindly at them? Can they successfully sail now on their route to a contested Republican Convention? Will they be able to continue to outwit the Trump Cyclops? Can the Republican sailors prevail against Trump and his electoral goats? Stay tuned, though in the end of the story, Odysseus does successfully maneuver past all sorts of monsters and gets to Ithaca, just as a growing number of opponents of Trump hope that happens now.

CHAPTER 5: BEWARE THE TRUMP WATER MONSTER

Trump is increasingly scaring everyone, as he is more and more seen as a fearsome monster who has to be stopped. For example, in a recent Huffington Post blog, Joe Selden wrote: "I now believe the anti-Trump movement has reached critical mass in the country, and that Trump – even if he is the Republican nominee – will not win the election. And he will have done so much damage to his brand, his party and the country, that he will not be easily forgiven, if forgiven at all."

It is in that spirit that I have been writing a series of articles comparing Trump to the many monsters in mythology who have terrorized many people. But often they have been defeated by a powerful hero, much like a James Bond of ancient times. I previously compared Trump to the dragon which St. George fights, to a Chimera, to a Cyclops, and to Medusa.

He might also be compared to the terrifying water monsters that can be found in many cultures – the Kelpie of the Irish, the Charybdis of the Greeks, and the Kraken of Norse mythology. These are all water beasts that have terrorized, captured, and devoured sailors, much like Trump has been terrorizing and destroying anyone who gets in his way, and most recently threatening that there might be violence if he is denied the nomination – though, of course, he isn't to blame if it happens. It will be his devoted minions who carry out his warnings of potential violence, much like the Nazi Stormtroopers tore through the cities of Europe, killing anyone deemed an enemy of the state.

The Kelpie is described by folklorists as a supernatural shape-shifting horse that haunts the rivers of Scotland, which might be especially fitting since Scotland is the scene of one of Trump's battles with the locals over building a golf course. Eventually, he beat down the opposition to build it. As the folktales go, the Kelpie could take many forms and had an insatiable appetite for eating humans. Most commonly it appeared like a beautiful tame horse standing by the riverside, so it appeared as a tempting ride for a tired traveler. But once anyone mounted the horse, they would find themselves in great danger, since the horse would rear and charge headlong into the deepest water and submerge with a noise like thunder, as it took each traveler to a watery grave. Or sometimes the Kelpie would appear like a hairy humanoid who lurked in the vegetation by the river, leapt out to attack passing travelers, and crushed the life out of anyone it grabbed.

Likewise, Trump seems to have a voracious appetite for taking on everybody and anybody, from Megyn Kelly and Marco Rubio, to large organizations like Univision and Fox News. Should anyone dare challenge him, he strikes back through his insulting words or lawyers, as in his effort to discredit Tarla Makaeff, a lead plaintiff in one of three suits against Trump University for fraud. Now she wants out, because she is so exhausted by the process of challenging Trump. Alternatively, like a tame horse, the Trumpie might appear very friendly, though it can turn on a dime, such as Trump's effort to at first praise and then discredit Ben Carson, when he was an opposing candidate, by calling him a child molester. But later Trump became the nice Trumpie again, when Carson came forward to endorse him and may even try to be his Vice President.

Yet the Kelpie does have its weak spot – it's Achilles' heel so to speak, although in this case it isn't his heel. Rather, the Kelpie's power of shapeshifting is claimed to come from its bridle, so anyone who could grab and hold onto the bridle could force the Kelpie to submit to their will. And supposedly one Scottish clan, the MacGregors, gained possession of a bridle, after one of their clan members saved himself from a Kelpie. After that they passed the bridle down from generation to generation,

So who can put the bridle on the Trumpie today? It would seem that Ted Cruz, John Kasich, and the Republican Party establishment are certainly trying; and Cruz has stepped up as the one to put on the bridle, as more and more Republican Party members are joining his campaign to defeat the Trumpie, while the media and even the online hacker group Anonymous have come forward to attack him, too. In fact, the Anonymous campaign to shut down Trump's websites sounds a little like a campaign to keep the Trumpie out of the virtual waters where he thrives, much like the MacGregors were able to stop the Kelpie's efforts to find his victims in the river waters, after one of the MacGregors grabbed the bridle and forced the Kelpie to submit to his will.

As for the other water monsters – the Charybdis of Greek mythology and the Kraken of the Norse myths, I'll describe the comparisons to Trump next.

CHAPTER 6: TRUMP AND THE MONSTERS OF THE SEA

Sailors have many tales of the dangers of the seas, which include vicious sea serpents and whirlpools. And for the terrors he strikes in many people today, Donald Trump might be compared to these dangerous creatures, such as the Kraken of Norse mythology and Charybdis, who has appeared in many Greek myths, including in the story of the Odyssey.

The Kraken is described in these myths as a huge sea monster that dwells off the coasts of Norway and Greenland, and perhaps the legend comes from sightings of giant squids that can be as large as 40 to 50 feet. The first references to the creature come from the late 13th century Old Iceland sagas, where it was called the "hafgufa." It was feared because of its many tentacles which could ensnare the masts of ships and drag them down to the icy ocean depths, and it could create a deadly whirlpool by submerging itself underwater to suck in the ships.

As one 13th century saga described it, the Kraken is "the hugest monster in the sea. It is the nature of this creature to swallow men and ships, and even whales and everything else within reach. It stays submerged for days, then rears its head and nostrils above the surface and stays that way at least until the change of tide." Later, Swedish author Jacob Wallenberg described the Kraken in 1781 thus: ""He stays at the sea floor, constantly surrounded by innumerable small fishes, who serve as his food and are fed by him in return…His excrements nurture in the following an army of lesser fish…Gradually, Kraken ascends to the surface, and when he is at ten to twelve fathoms, the boats had better move out of his vicinity, as he will shortly thereafter burst up, like a floating island, spurting water from his dreadful nostrils and making ring waves around him, which can reach many miles. Could one doubt that this is the Leviathan of Job?" The Kraken even appears in Melville's 1851 novel *Moby Dick,* when the Pequod encounters a great live squid compared to the great Kraken.

    As for Charybdis of Greek mythology, she sounds much like the Kraken. Originally, she was a water nymph and goddess of the tide, who was too successful in carrying out the wishes of Poseidon, her sea god father, in riding the storms onto the land to flood towns, forests, and beaches. As a result, Zeus grew furious about her claims on the land and turned her into a sea monster – a huge fat beast with a giant mouth. Then, he chained her to the bottom of the sea in the Strait of Messina. There, three times a day, she continued to suck down water from the sea and spit it out to create the tides, but she also swallowed anything that got caught in her whirlpool. As a result, when Odysseus on his voyage back to Ithaca had to choose between sailing by Charybdis or Scylla, a sea monster in a larger rock, he preferred to risk the death of some of his men to Scylla than all of them to Charybdis.

    Trump has many parallels with both mythical monsters. Much like the Kraken with his huge tentacles, Trump has his tentacles everywhere in his many real estate and other businesses. Also, like both the Kraken and Charybdis, he swallows up and drags down those who get in his way, from other businessmen to politicians. Among other things, Trump has taken the land of those opposing his expansion through eminent domain, such as when he attempted to take the land of Vera Coking, an elderly widow, in Atlanta City to build a limousine parking lot for the Trump Plaza hotel, though he eventually lost, as described in a blog by Neo-Neocon, "Donald Trump loves the regular folks – unless their homes happen to stand in Trump's way."   Additionally, Trump sought to condemn five small businesses so he could build an office and entertainment complex in Bridgeport, Connecticut, and won, as Ilya Somin describes in "Donald Trump's history of domain abuse". In Scotland, he tried to similarly push local homeowners out of their homes to build his golf course, insulting many of the property owners, such as calling one man "the village idiot" and claiming he "lives like a pig." Plus, there are the many media people and politicians who he has attempted to insult or destroy, like the Kraken or Charybdis swallowing up passing ships, if they opposed him.

      Thus, much like the sailors of yore, many politicians have tried to get out of Trump's way, so they aren't pulled under by his tentacles, but now a growing number of opponents have joined forces to take him down. More and more media voices are speaking out, while many Republican Party establishment members are coming forward to oppose him and support another candidate, in order to avoid the dangers of the Trump Kraken or Charybdis.

CHAPTER 7: TRUMP AND THE MANY HEADED MONSTERS

Many monsters in myths have several heads, making them even more dangerous, which might be compared to the many hats Trump wears as the head of a real estate empire, a reality show host, owner of multiple companies with the Trump brand, and now a presidential campaign.

Previously, I compared Trump to the dragon St. George fights, to a Chimera, to the Medusa, to the fearsome horse monster of Scotland, the Kelpie, and to two monsters of the sea, the Kraken and Charybdis.

Now there are two more monsters with multiple heads that might be compared to Trump – the Hydra, a serpent-like water monster with nine or so heads, and Cerberus, the guardian of Hades, with three or more heads. Both were among the twelve labors of Heracles, which he carried out as a penance over 12 years for King Eurystheus, due to killing his own wife, son and daughter in a fit of insanity. But in return for atoning for his actions, as the Oracle of Delphi advised him, he would be rewarded with immortality. In any event, Heracles' second labor was to kill the nine-headed Hyrda and his sixth was to capture and bring back Cerberus. Both were considered especially deadly monsters, so that's why Heracles was asked to kill or capture them for the king.

The Hydra, a serpent-like water monster with reptilian characteristics, was considered extremely dangerous because of its deadly venom. Its breath could be lethal to anyone who came near, and it could quickly regrow any of its decapitated limbs. Moreover, if any of its heads were severed, apart from its central core head, two more would grow in their place. The Hydra was elusive, too, since it hid in Lake Lerna in an underwater cave that some considered an entrance to the underworld. At first, Heracles seemed to have an impossible battle. Initially, he covered his mouth and nose with cloth to remain safe from the Hydra's deadly fumes from its many mouths when he attacked the Hydra with a sickle, sword, or club. But that attack didn't work very well, since each time he lopped off a head, the Hydra grew two more. . However, with a little help from his nephew Iolaus, he found success. After he cut off each head, Iolaus cauterized the open stump with a torch, and the Hydra couldn't produce anymore heads. Then, Heracles was finally able to kill the Hydra by cutting off its last head.

As for Cerberus, this was the huge hound with three heads that guarded the entrance to Hades, the underworld. Supposedly, the beast only liked to eat living flesh, so he would consume any living mortal who came near him, while allowing the deceased spirits to pass by. As the story goes, Heracles had to get Hades' permission to bring Cerberus to the surface, and Hades agreed if Heracles could subdue the beast without any weapons. So Heracles did, using his great strength to overpower the hound with his hands. Then, he carried the beast over his back, dragged him to the surface, and brought him back to King Eurystheus. But the king was so terrified that he begged Heracles to return the hound of hell back to Hades, which he did. And after that, Eurystheus agreed to release Heracles from any further labors.

Well, in this case, the comparison certainly fits for Trump and both monsters. Trumps' insults and humiliating words might be compared to the Hydra's deadly venom, and Trump uses his words to attack his many enemies through Tweets, put-downs at press conferences, and calls at his rallies, such as when he yells out "Get him outta here," to his security guards, who promptly throw out the victim. Also, it seems that whenever someone attacks Trump with one claim, like pointing to his failed Trump University, Trump fights back, like growing another head, such as by calling the attacker a loser or having his lawyers tie up the opponent, if threatening enough, with litigation in court. Likewise, the way Trump has destroyed other candidates, such as Jeb Bush, by calling him low energy; Ben Carson, by tagging him as a child molester; or Marco Rubio, by mocking him as Little Rubio for his little experience, low attendance record in the Senate, and being short, might be compared to the Cerberus eating living mortals. As for Cerberus' willingness to let the deceased spirits go through the gates of Hades, that might be comparable to Trump's embrace of anyone who supports him, even the often languid Ben Carson, who some have compared to the living dead, because he often seems so lethargic and seems to have sold his soul to get on Trump's good side, with a view to becoming a cabinet member, such as the Secretary of Education, or even a VP.

So now it would seem the world is waiting for its modern day Heracles – also called Hercules by the Romans, after the Roman Empire captured Greece and the Romans transformed the Greek myths into their own. Might it be Ted Cruz or John Kasich, who have engaged in difficult labors on the campaign trail? Or perhaps if they can't do it, Hillary Clinton or Bernie Sanders can, and they have both similarly engaged in many labors all over the country in their many stops in what has become an especially long arduous campaign.

CHAPTER 8: TRUMP AND THE HUMAN BEASTS

Besides the deadly animal monsters, some of the most fearsome monsters in myths combine the heads and bodies of humans and animals, including raging bulls and lions, so they are very wily and bloodthirsty – just like Donald Trump, who I have compared to other beasts.

Three of the most feared human beasts are the Minotaur, which has the head of a bull and the body of a man; the Manticore, which has the body of a lion, the head of a man, and the stinging tail of a scorpion; and the Sphinx, which also has the body of a lion, but has the head of a woman and the wings of an eagle.

The Minotaur was the ferocious offspring of a woman and beast, after Minos' queen slept with a bull, and he devoured humans for his sustenance. Embarrassed by the creature, King Minos hid him in the Labyrinth at the Minoan Palace of Knossos. There the Minotaur lived on regular sacrificial offerings of youths and young maidens, and since the labyrinth was such a complicated construction, no one could find their way out alive. However, after King Minos decided to kill the Minotaur, Theseus volunteered to do so to end the human sacrifices. But could he find his way out? He learned how after the king's daughter, Princess Ariadne, fell madly in love with him and gave him a thread to unravel. So Theseus followed the thread into the Labyrinth and used it to get out after he killed the monster. In this case, the labyrinth might be compared to the maze of Trump's many real estate holdings and companies that are run by many different managers and involve so many complicated financial arrangements that the IRS has been doing a series of audits to figure everything out. And all the people the Minotaur has eaten could be comparable to all of the property and company owners Trump trampled to obtain his land and companies, as well as to the candidates he gobbled up along the way to become the candidate with the most votes.

Though the Manticore got its start in India, it became part of Greek mythology due to the writings of Ctesias, a Greek physician who stayed at the court of the Persian king Artaxerxes II Menemon from 404 to 398/397 B.C. and wrote a book about India. As the legend goes, the Manticore had three rows of teeth like a shark, a bellow like a trumpet, and the ability to shoot spines from its tail. But most terrifying of all, it loved to eat human flesh. It would run quickly to chase down its prey, slash them with its claws, sting with its spiny tail, and finally eat them, devouring even their bones, clothes, and all of their possessions, leaving nothing for anyone to find. Additionally, Ctesia claimed, the Manticore could even paralyze or kill its victims from a distance by firing stingers from its tail, like a hunter with a bow. Now that description might sound a little like Trump at one of his rallies, which are becoming more and more violent, as he bellows out his comments and yells "Get 'em out of here" to his security people that rough up and eject anyone who appears to be a foe. Also, Trump's love of ripping enemies apart verbally, such as his diatribes against Megan Kelly and Ted Cruz, is like the way the Manticore tears apart and eats up a victim.

  As for the Sphinx, it is best known from the legend of Oedipus. As the story goes, Oedipus was traveling along the road to Thebes, when a sphinx appeared and blocked his path, asking him a riddle. Although the exact riddle isn't stated in the original legend, it is most commonly described as this: "What is that which goes on four feet in the morning, on two feet in the afternoon, and on three in the evening?" If Oedipus couldn't answer correctly, the sphinx would have strangled and eaten him, just as ate many other travelers. But Oedipus correctly answers, explaining that it's man, who crawls on all fours as a child; on two feet as an adult, and finally, with the help of a cane, on three feet at the end of his life. So since Oedipus has answered correctly, he has bested the Sphinx at her own game, so she throws herself from a high cliff, or in some versions, she devours herself in anger and frustration.
  Again, some comparisons with Trump seem apt. He certainly expects certain kinds of responses from people, or otherwise he calls out: "You're fired!" or "Get out of here." He has also been eating up much of the competition, as candidate after candidate has disappeared from the race, until there were two plus

the Trump Sphinx. However, so far, those two candidates – Ted Cruz and John Kasich have been giving enough right answers to the media and to many voters, so they have remained in the race, and a brokered convention is likely. Should that happen, Trump has likely been bested at his own game, and like the Sphinx he could end up being thrown from the modern day high cliff. And what's that? Well, it could be having his own brand tarnished from his appeals to racism, bigotry, xenophobia, and hatred, which have turned millions of people against him and have led to growing protests at his events.

But while Theseus managed to kill the Minotaur and find his way out of the labyrinth, can a modern-day Theseus, such as Ted Cruz, John Kasich, Hillary Clinton, or Bernie Sanders, do the same? And what will happen to the Trump Manticore or Trump Sphinx? In the myths, the fate of the humans against the Manticore is less certain, but Oedipus correctly knows how to defeat the Sphinx at her own game. And perhaps a modern-day Oedipus like Kasich or Cruz may do the same.

CHAPTER 9: IS TRUMP THE MODERN-DAY DEVIL?

Many religions and cultures have a belief in the devil, viewed as a being who personifies evil and is the most fearsome enemy of God and humankind. This devil or demon is known by many names – the Dybbuk in Jewish mythology; Beelzebub, Lucifer, or Satan for Christians, Iblis or Azazel for Muslims believers in Islam; and Mephistopheles, a demon in German folklore. Today, for a growing legion of people, Donald Trump has become the modern devil, because of his association with racism, bigotry, xenophobia, inciting violence, lying about almost everything, and otherwise having the attributes of someone who is a dangerous threat to humanity.

I previously compared Trump to the dragon St. George fights, to a Chimera, to a Cyclops, and to Medusa. I have also compared him to the Kelpie horse monster of Scotland, to the Kraken and Charybdis monsters of the sea, to the many-headed Hydra and Cerberus, and to the half-human beasts, the Minotaur, Manticore, and Sphinx. Given all these parallels with other monsters, can one compare Trump to the most evil monster of all – the devil or demon in his many forms? Certainly, it would seem that one can.

First, take the Dybbuk, who is called the Jewish version of a demon and was first written about in the 16th century. The Dybbuk is a malicious spirit who takes possession of the souls of good, honest people and causes them to engage in destructive acts and mayhem. According to this tradition, the Dybbuk is the dislocated soul of a dead person who wreaks havoc on a living person and leaves the body once it has accomplished its goal. In effect, one becomes possessed by this evil spirit, leading one to do terrible things, as in "the devil made me do it."

As for the devil, in the Christian tradition, by whatever name he is called – Beelzebub, Lucifer, or Satan, the devil is sometimes considered one of the seven princes of Hell, according to the Catholic tradition. Commonly, he is believed to fight God over the souls of humans and command a force of evil spirits, commonly known as demons. As Satan, he is often identified as the serpent who convinced Eve to eat the forbidden apple, as described in the Book of Revelations, and he is sometimes called Lucifer who became a fallen angel, when thrown out of heaven, as described in Isaiah. While Beelzebub was once the name of a Philistine god, this name was used in the New Testament as a synonym for Satan.

Finally, Mephistopheles was originally a demon in German folklore. But in the 16th century, this name became associated with the Faust legend, which was based on a real historic figure, Johann Georg Faust, an alchemist, astrologer, and magician of the German Renaissance, who lived from about 1466 to 1541. After he died in an explosion of an alchemical experiment, a popular tale began circulating that the devil came to collect him, since he had engaged in various types of fraud and blasphemy, so the church denounced him as in league with the devil. Then, his name became part of a series of works of Faustian literature based on the story of a scholar who wagers his soul with the devil and loses.

Thus, given this historical backdrop, might Trump be considered the modern-day devil – or at least a person who has sold his soul to the devil for fame, power, and glory? It seems a very apt comparison, because in many ways in which Trump has taken the souls of his followers like the Dybbuk. Moreover, he has been battling a great many people and even God, when he criticized the Pope for visiting the border between Mexico and the U.S., and the Pope suggested Trump was not Christian, because of the harshness of his campaign promise to deport more immigrants and force Mexico to pay for a wall along the border. Then, too, the growing hordes of followers at his rallies, especially those who act violently against others or raise their hands in a Nazi-like salute of loyalty, might be compared to the force of evil spirits commanded by the devil. And the efforts of some countries, such as Britain, to ban him, might be compared to the actions of God in throwing Lucifer out of heaven, so he becomes a fallen angel.

Finally, Trump might be compared to the serpent tempting Eve in the way he has spent lavishly to show off his luxury homes, hotels, and golf courses, which provide a great temptation for the wealthy. But then, employing the wiles of a serpent, he has used the power of eminent domain to push the poor people living in the way of his expanding domains out of the way, while he has used many poor workers from other countries to build these homes, hotels, and golf courses.

But if Trump is comparable to a modern-day devil, who will take him on? Who will throw him out of heaven for good? Perhaps it's time for writers, politicians, government officials, and others working towards a better future to find a way to open the door and say, "Get him outta here," as Trump would say to others.

PART II: CHILDREN'S STORIES FOR ADULTS

THE BATTLES OF DONNIE AND TEDDY
4 Children's Stories about the 2016 Election for Adults

INTRODUCTION

THE BATTLES OF DONNIE AND TEDDY was inspired by watching the Republican Party debates, and especially the knock-down drag out fight between Donald Trump and Ted Cruz. The election campaign was already getting ugly, when a Super Pac for Ted put a picture of Melenia Trump, a former model, from a 15 year-old photo shoot looking very sexy with the words: "Meet Your New First Lady."

Though Cruz denied having anything to do with this ad, Trump didn't believe him, and returned fire with two photos of Cruz's wife, Heidi, a Harvard MBA, economist, and former Goldman Sachs investment analyst. The photo on left showed her looking like a disheveled drunk on a bender, next to a recent photo on the right where she looked very distinguished.

Then, after the Internet world went wild about the growing fight between Trump and Cruz getting dirtier and dirtier now that their wives were subject to attack, things got even scummier with an article in the *National Enquirer,* apparently placed by one of Trump's operatives, which claimed that Cruz had five secret mistresses. Cruz quickly claimed the story was garbage, while Trump said he had nothing to do with the article, though the *National Enquirer* was right before as the first to report several high profile scandals.

And so the fight goes on, while the Republican Party is appalled, as are many national leaders, who have expressed concern that the level of personal attacks are not befitting a Presidential candidate, much less a President, and are dragging down the reputation of the U.S. into the mud.

Meanwhile, I kept thinking of the continuing battles of Trump and Cruz as much like two little boys in kindergarten or first grade fighting. They hurl insults, call each other names, and try to humiliate one another and his family members. They are like two little boys in a sandbox, fighting over a piece of cake, trying to get a toy from the other, calling each other names, and fighting with fists or available objects to ultimately be the victor.

So I have written this book in that spirit – featuring Trump and Cruz as two little kids fighting – and then fighting some more. At this point, I'm not sure who will win, or maybe neither will, since other kids or some adults seeing them fight may kick them out. And maybe that'll happen in the real battle between Trump and Cruz if they knock each other out, so no one will win, and some other kid from the party or another party will become the new champion.

The book features four stories of two kids fighting – in the sandbox, at a birthday party, at the lake, and at the playground. So let the battles begin.

IN THE SANDBOX

Donnie was building castles in the sandbox, when Mrs. Marple came over with Teddy, who was carrying a pail with a shovel.

"Donnie," she said, "Teddy just moved here with his mother and sister, and he would like to join you."

"No," Donnie said. "I don't want him to play here." He glared at Teddy and Mrs. Marple.

Teddy looked scared, but Mrs. Marple pushed him forward.

"That's not very nice, Donnie," Mrs. Marple said. "You have to learn to play with the other children."

Donnie stood up very tall. He pushed out his chest. "I don't want to," he said.

"But you have to do this," Mrs. Marple said. "Otherwise the other children won't like you."

"I don't care," Donnie said. "I don't like them very much either."

"You have to learn to get along with others," Mrs. Marple replied. "So I'm going to leave Teddy here with you. You have to learn to play together."

Mrs. Marple guided Teddy into the sandbox. As she did, Teddy stuck out his tongue at Donnie. "So there," he said.

Donnie glared back Teddy as hard as he could. But Teddy didn't flinch. Instead, he sat down in the far corner of the sandbox. He started building a castle, too.

But before he could finish his castle, Donnie stood up and kicked it over. The sand went flying.

"You can't build another castle here," Donnie said. "I won't let you. "

"Who says," said Teddy. "I'll tell Mrs. Marple on you, and she'll come back and help me. She likes me better."

"So what?" said Donnie. "I'm stronger than you."

Donnie reached out and punched Teddy. Teddy fell back for a moment. Then, he tried to punch Donnie again, but Donnie punched him back.

"Ha, ha!" Donnie laughed. "You see. You're not up to it. I'm the only one who can build castles here."

"No, I can, too," Teddy yelled. "Besides, if you don't let me play, I know some things about you, and I'll tell."

"Oh, yeah," Donnie yelled back. "You're the new kid on the block, and I bet no one likes you either."

"Well, once they know what you're really like, no one will like you either."

"So you think you're a know it all. But you're lying. You're Lying Crying Teddy," Donnie jeered.

"No, I'm not," Teddy screamed back. "Because I heard a lot of other kids say this. Your mother's an alien from another planet, and your sister has cooties."

"What? That's not fair," Donnie said. "You can't insult my mother and sister."

"But I can. I can," Teddy laughed. "Maybe you're better at throwing punches. But I'm better at insults."

"Oh, no, you're not. Because if you're going to get in the mud, I will, too."

Donnie grabbed a pile of dirt at the side of the sandbox and threw it at Teddy. It splattered all over his face and dripped down his shirt.

"So, there," said Donnie. "And you know what? I heard about your own mother and sister, too. Your mother's like a dog, an ugly stupid mutt. And your sister's a crazy little runt who was in the pound after her owner threw her in the gutter."

Teddy got up, holding his shovel like a knife.

"Oh, no you don't," he yelled and charged at Donnie.

But Donnie quickly blew himself up to twice his size. He picked up a baseball bat and swung at Teddy.

But Teddy ducked. He picked up a pail of sand and threw it at Donnie.

Donnie stepped back away from the spray of sand and blew himself up even more. He began breathing out flames like a dragon.

Teddy ducked again, but Donnie kicked him and then kicked him again. He began to laugh and point hysterically.

"There! See, I've got you. I'm the strongest one of all." He beat on his chest, like the king of the jungle.

Just then, Mrs. Marple came running out.

"Oh, boys. Boys. You mustn't fight. That's against school rules. The principal and all the teachers will be furious."

Donnie and Teddy backed away from each other and sat down opposite ends of the sandbox. Donnie sat beside what was left of his castle; Teddy sat beside his turned-over pail.

Mrs. Marple continued. "I had hoped you could play together. We all had such high hopes for you. But now that's over. Since you can't play nicely together and follow the rules, you are both suspended."

Donnie and Teddy look up, shocked.

"But you can't throw me out," Donnie cried.

"Oh, but I can," Mrs. Marple said. "Now you both have to go home. You can't play in the sandbox anymore."

At once Donnie deflated to his original size, and Teddy began sobbing. Mrs. Marple just glared at them.

Then, they both left the sandbox walking in different directions. There was nothing left to be said.

AT THE BIRTHDAY PARTY

Mrs. Jonas brought out a big chocolate birthday cake and put it on the backyard picnic table.

A dozen children at the party lined up to get some. Donnie pushed to the head of the line, Teddy right behind him.

Donnie held out his plate. Teddy tried to push him aside.

"You pushed ahead of me," Teddy claimed.

"No, I didn't," Donnie exclaimed. "You were behind me."

"But you pushed me out of the way."

"No, I didn't," Donnie said.

"But you did," Teddy said.

Mrs. Jonas came over to them. "Now, don't fight, boys. Just wait your turn. There's plenty of cake for everyone."

She gave Donnie a slice of cake, and then gave one to Teddy.

As they walked off, Donnie held up his plate of cake. "Mine's bigger," he said.

Teddy looked at his plate, and indeed his slice was smaller.

"Well, not for long," Teddy said, and he pushed Donnie.

Donnie started to slip. His plate of cake teetered and tottered. It looked like it was about to fall off, when he grabbed onto a nearby chair to steady himself.

"Now who's the loser?" Donnie said.

He pushed Teddy back. Teddy's plate started to tilt and his cake slid to the edge, when he grabbed it back.

"No, I'm not," Teddy yelled, pushing his plate with his cake against Donnie's chest. "There, you see!" he exclaimed.

Donnie began to fall, and his cake nearly fell off his plate, but he caught himself.

"You see. I still have the biggest piece of cake."

Hearing Donnie's boast, Teddy became even madder. He lifted his plate and smashed his cake into Donnie's face.

"Well, if you want the biggest piece, take this."

The cake splattered all over Donnie's face, and he dropped his cake into the mud.

"You slimy weasel," Donnie yelled. "Now my cake is all full of dirt."

"And so are you!" Teddy yelled back.

"And you are, too, you snake," Donnie yelled, and pushed Teddy into the mud.

"Now you're all dirty, too."

Soon they both were rolling around in the mud, getting dirtier and dirtier, like two dinosaurs fighting, while their cake was also covered with mud.

Just then Mrs. Jonas came over.

"Boys, boys, you can't fight here. This is a nice birthday party."

Donnie and Teddy stopped fighting for a moment.

"But we're not fighting now," Donnie said.

"We'll be good," Teddy said.

"No, I'm sorry," Mrs. Jonas replied. "You've already ruined the party with your fighting. All the other children are very embarrassed. So you'll have to leave."

Donnie and Teddy got up and went out the gate. Mrs. Jonas watched them go, and the other children finished getting their cake. Then, they sat down at the tables, talking and smiling, glad that Donnie and Teddy were gone.

Meanwhile, on the road, Donnie and Teddy began fighting again. They each found a toy sword on the side of the road and began swinging at each other.

Suddenly, Teddy screamed. "Don't hit me so hard, you don't fight fair."

But Donny just laughed. "See, I won again. You're such a loser. Loser! Loser! Loser!" he yelled.

That made Teddy really mad. So even if Donnie seemed stronger, he was so mad, he was determined to fight back. So he jumped back up, and started hitting Teddy even harder.

Whap! Whap! Bam! Bam! They hit each other again and again.

But after they both fell down, Donnie jumped up and went running down the road. Soon Teddy ran after him.

"You'll never catch me," Donnie called out.

"Oh, yes I will," Teddy yelled back.

When Teddy finally caught up in town, they began fighting some more. After a while, a dog stopped by and looked on quietly, wondering what the fight was about and who would win.

Meanwhile, as they kept fighting and fighting, and then running and running and fighting some more, in the backyard, all the other children were enjoying the party, glad that Donnie and Teddy were gone.

AT THE LAKE

Donnie was eager to go to the lake and try out his new toys.

He imagined all the things he could do. He could play with his ball and kick it as hard as he could. Whenever he won a goal, everyone would cheer, and he could once again say: "I'm a winner. I'm the best."

Or he could imagine he was a knight battling the feared Minotaur, and, of course, he would win like he always did. For once he got ready for battle, the enemy would have no chance, and there were always enemies to defeat.

Then, when he won and could once again say those magic words: "I'm the greatest!" and "Be gone! You're outta here."

Or maybe he could try out his new toy tank. He liked it because it was the biggest and best tank, and it was perfect for shooting down anyone who opposed him or was out to get him, such as that new kid on the block, Teddy, who was trying to take him down.

Also, he liked this new tank, since now the other kids would like and admire him even more, because it showed he was so tough and strong. So now they would follow him wherever he wanted to take them.

And he was sure more kids would follow him than Teddy, since almost nobody liked Teddy, because he lied and cheated so much and had a big nose, just like Pinocchio.

But for now, Donnie just wanted to think of all the ways he could show he was the best. And if he had to scare a few kids into believing that, well, it was fun to scare them, too.

Then, as he looked back into the lake, he imagined what it might like to be a fish. There were so many hooks and other obstacles to avoid. But if he was smart, he could avoid them and show he was the biggest fish there, too.

"You just have to know not to take the bait, so it's best to swim fast and be very elusive," he thought. "That way no one could catch up to me or catch me up."

But as he was thinking of how great he was and all the great things he could do, Sally from his school came by. She always tried in class to show how smart she was, so the teacher and the other kids would like her. Well, he would show her.

So he began yelling at her: "You're fat. You're ugly. You look like a fat pig. You think you're smart and pretty, but you're pretty dumb. And you think everyone likes you, but they really don't. They're just pretending they think you're nice, but they really hate you."

At that Sally started to cry, but Donnie didn't want to stop. He was enjoying tormenting her too much.

"There, see. You can't take it. You're just a stupid girl. So go home to mommy and daddy. Maybe they'll take care of you or maybe not. If they don't think you're good enough, maybe they'll give you away."

And Sally cried even more.

After Sally ran home, Donnie saw Teddy coming to the lake. At first, he tried to scare Teddy off by teasing him: "You're like a monkey. Monkey see. Monkey do."

He moved his arms up and down, scratched his head, and jumped up around like a monkey."

"And just like a monkey, you try to copy what I do. Plus you're a thief, too, 'cause you're trying to steal my friends away. Well, you can't, and that's not fair."

"No, no. I'm not doing that. I'm just trying to get to know people and get along," Teddy protested.

He even began begging Donnie not to be mad at him and hurt him.

"Can't we still be friends," he said.

But Donnie didn't want to be friends. No, not at all. For now he was sure Teddy wanted to become number one himself after moving to his town. And he couldn't have that.

So he pushed Teddy back into the grass.

Teddy fell down and a moment later he screamed: "I've been bitten by a snake."

But Donnie just laughed, and jeered at Teddy some more.

So Teddy became madder at Donnie than ever. He grabbed a pot from a nearby picnic table and put it on his head to ward off any blows. Then he began punching at Donnie, and Donnie began punching him back.

Suddenly, a park ranger appeared.

"You can't fight here," he said.

At first, Donnie and Teddy didn't listen. They kept on fighting.

But when another park ranger came over, they thought it was better to stop fighting, at least for now.

But they both knew the fight wasn't over yet. So they left the park yelling and screaming at each other.

"You're a liar and a thief," said Donnie.

"You're a snake and weasel," said Teddy.

"Well, I'll tell on your secrets," said Donnie.

"And I'll tell everyone how horrible and terrible you are," said Teddy. "You're like a big bad wolf, and you've got a big fat head like a pumpkin."

"And you're like the devil himself," said Donnie.

So they kept arguing and yelling at each other as they walked home from the lake. Each was trying to come up with more and better insults than the other.

Then, it began to rain, and they walked their separate ways out of the park after that.

AT THE PLAYGROUND

When Donnie came to the playground with his mother and sister Maria, he saw playing on the swings, slide, and teeter-totter.

"What fun," he thought, eager to meet the other kids, since he always liked to make new friends. He had some great ideas for new games they could play with him.

Then, he saw Teddy coming to the park with his sister Harriet, and he became upset. Why did Teddy have to be here and ruin his wonderful day?

Donnie was mad at Teddy for taking some of his marbles, when they played together a few days before.

So he went over to Teddy and yelled at him.
"You stole my marbles."
"No, I didn't," said Teddy.
"You're a liar," said Donnie. "A thief and a liar."
"No, I'm not," said Teddy.
"You are," said Donnie.
"Not," said Teddy.

Their argument went back and forth, until Donnie pointed a short stubby finger at him and screamed:

"There you go again, you lying Teddy."

Donnie jumped up and down and continued to chant, like he was playing a gotcha game: "Lying Teddy! Lying Teddy! Lying Teddy!"

He stomped his feet three times, as if that would make Teddy go away and disappear.

Teddy responded with surprise, a little scared by Donnie's jumping and chanting.

"What would Donnie do next?" he wondered. "And could Donnie really hurt him?

"Well, you're just a great big bully," Teddy yelled back. He even dropped the ice cream cone he had been eating.

But being called a bully made Donnie feel even stronger. So he blew himself up some more, glad to see that Teddy was afraid of him, like many other kids.

"I can even punch them and beat them up, and they still follow me," he thought, because I'm so much stronger than everyone else.

Suddenly, Teddy noticed Donnie's sister Maria standing nearby laughing at him.

So he got even madder.

"Well, you may think you're so great, but your sister is stupid and ugly," he yelled.

"No, she isn't," Donnie yelled back. "Everyone thinks she's very beautiful."

"Then, she's still very stupid. And she's dumb to have you as a brother."

At once, Maria began crying, and Donnie got madder and madder.

"You can't insult my sister like that," Donnie said. "It's not fair."

"Well, you aren't fair," Teddy said.

"It takes one to call one," Donnie said. "Monkey see, monkey do.

Then, seeing Teddy's sister nearby, he told Teddy, "If you can insult my sister, I can insult your sister even more.   Just watch."

He began calling Harriet all kinds of names.

"You look like a fat pig."

"You are fat like a hippo."

"And all the kids think of you as a dumb stupid clown. So you should go back to your box and go away."

At this, Harriet began to cry, too.

"You can't treat my sister like this," Teddy yelled.
"You started it," said Donnie. "You called my sister names first."
"No, I didn't. I just said what the other kids said."

"Oh, yeah," said Donnie, getting madder and madder, so his face soon looked like a big orange ball.

Donnie began punching Teddy, and Teddy punched him back.

Whap! Bam! The fight went on and on.

Meanwhile, the other kids in the playground gathered around to watch.

They began clapping and cheering, like they were watching a prize fight, and picking on their favorite to win.

Donnie felt great with all the attention he was getting. He loved being in the spotlight and hearing all the fans on his side cheering him on, while the others were just losers.

And Teddy just wanted to win. So he kept fighting harder and harder, determined to finally beat Donnie at his own game.

But just as Teddy was getting ready for what he thought would be a knock-out blow, a teacher from the school next door came rushing over.

"You can't fight like this, children. You have to stop."

For a moment, Teddy held his arm in the air. He so wanted to smash Donnie's face and show he could win. But then he heard the teacher calling out even louder:

"You have to stop! You have to stop right now, and you have to leave at once. You are embarrassing the school. You can't act like this.

So, Teddy got up, and then Donnie did, too.

"Now leave," the teacher said. "And don't come back until you are ready to behave. No more fighting. No more name calling. You have to play nicely together, or you can't come back."

So both Donnie and Teddy and their sisters left, going in different directions. But they still thought about what they might do in the future to show the other who was really the greatest of them all.

PART III: CARTOON BOOKS

Illustrated by Nick Alexander

TRUMP IS EXTINCT…OR MAY BE SOON!

An Illustrated Guide Featuring Trump as 27 Extinct Beasts and Early Humans

INTRODUCTION

This book is dedicated to the many opponents who would like to see Trump defeated and the end to his Presidential campaign. They feel Trump's campaign has been based on insults, humiliation, and inciting his followers to violence. He has been called a bigot and racist and compared to Hitler. Some have considered him a dangerous evil monster.

In the past, many dangerous and scary beasts have gone extinct, so this book has been created in this spirit of comparing Trump to many now extinct beasts, including early humans and a new Trump species that is sure to go extinct as many hope.

Each of these profiles features a portrait of these different extinct creatures, along with a brief description.

DINOSAURS

The Trumposaurus (aka the 6 foot 70 pound Coelursaurus from Wyoming in the Upper Jurassic) is truly a fearsome beast, with the kill, kill, kill instincts of a carnivore. Who will he go after next? Just about anyone or anything that gets in the way of his massive teeth.

Trumposaurus

The Tyrannosaurus Trump (aka the 40 foot 8 ton Tyrannosaurus Rex, who roamed the flood plains, swamps, and forests of Montana and Alberta in the late Cretaceous), eagerly eats up anything he can overpower. He enjoys seeing his prey cower in terror or run in fear. Then, when he captures and swallows them up, he feels even more power and is ready to conquer, kill, and eat his next meal.

Tryannosaurus Trump

The Trumporaptor (aka the 8 foot 150 pound Velociraptor, who roamed Mongolia and Eastern Asia during the Upper Cretaceous) is known for slicing and dicing his prey with his long claw on each hind foot that cuts like a knife. Just some kind words and flattery are all he needs to draw his latest victims under his spell. Then, zap! Each victim is caught underfoot like a cult follower eager to follow anywhere, as the Trumporapter raps on. Then, the Trumporaptor is on to the next victim to satisfy his rapacious hunger.

Trumporaptor

The Spinotrumpus (aka the 30 foot 3 ton Spinosaurus, a meat-eating scavenger from the floodplains of Egypt during the Upper Cretaceous) is well-known for putting a spin on things. So whenever challenged, he can easily spin things around and change direction on a dime. Or as necessary, he can play nice, then spin around and launch an attack when least expected. Or if a competitor or the media tries to spin anything, he can spin away and rebound with another attack that can put anyone in a tailspin – so they're spinning, spinning, spinning, until they crash and burn. And then the Spinotrumpus can spin on to find the next victim to play the spinning game.

Spinotrumpus

The Brontotrumpus (aka the 80 foot 30 ton Brontosaurus from Wyoming, Utah, and Colorado in the Upper Jurassic) loves to roam around the flood plains and lakes munching on anything green – from grass and leafy plants to lots of cash. He especially likes munching on the media and anyone who gets in his way, and he has attracted a big following who feast on everything he excretes along the path.

Brontotrumpus

The Stegotrumpus (aka the 30 ton 20 foot Stegosaurus, a plant-eater from Wyoming, Utah, and Colorado during the Upper Jurassic), is always ready to defend itself at the slightest opportunity. It uses its big tail to slap and whap anyone who dares attack. So should anyone come after it, it is eager to strike back with all it's got, using everything from threats to charging and charging some more, until any would-be predators slink away, afraid to make the Stegotrumpus even madder and more deadly.

Stegotrumpus

The Iguanoramus Trump (aka the 30 foot 6 ton plant-eating Iguanodon, who frequented the swamps and lakes of England and Belgium during the Lower Cretaceous) was known for fighting fierce and dirty with the large menacing spikes on his front feet to fight off rivals and to defend against predators. But unfortunately, he had an Achilles heel, or perhaps more accurately, Iguanoramus heel in that he just didn't know what he didn't know, so he was really an ignoramus, though of course, he didn't want to admit this. Rather, he wanted others to think he knew what he didn't know by talking as loud and as fast as he could, but after a while, his charm wore off, as others realized he was just an ignoramus Iguanoramus.

Iguanoramos Trumpus

The Trumpatops (aka the 30 foot 6 ton Triceratops, from the flood plains and swamp forests of Wyoming, Montana, and Alberta during the Upper Cretaceous) may seem like a peaceful vegetarian, but watch out! If anyone poses a threat, he's aggressive in protecting his herd of followers and is willing, ready, and able to confront just about anyone about anything. So he's known for being scrappy and pugnacious, unwilling to take anything from anyone, while he gives out whatever he wants, and he supports the team around him when they strike out at anyone who comes too close. Also, it uses its deadly horns to fight, fight, fight, like a wound up trap ready to spring once anything startles it, so others beware its fury, or else.

Trumpatops

The Anklytrumpus (aka the 15 foot 3 ton Anklyosaurus, another plant-eater, from the Alberta and Mongolia lowland swamps and rivers of the Upper Cretaceous) is known for lying in wait like a fortress protected by his heavy armor of spikes, and then should any enemy come too near, wham! He attacks with a heavy club at the end of his tail, though he can easily bring in reinforcements with their own clubs to strike any challengers and chase them away. In fact, he is known to be so fearless, that he is ready to fight off or take on any small predators, such as a young Tyrannosaurus Kasich that wandered into its path, only to be swatted away. And now he is gearing up to ward off still more foes, though eventually, if too many foes attack, he might finally retreat, while doing as much damage as he can with his armor of spite…er spikes.

Anklyotrumpus vs. Tyrannus Kasich

The Hadrotrumpus (aka the Hadrosauraus, a 30 foot, 3-4 ton plant eater from the New Jersey swamps during the Late Cretaceous) can run fast on his hind legs when necessary, though he mostly runs on all fours. It all depends on whether he's running away, which is happening more and more these days, or running to or for something, though no one's really sure which way he is running, since he's constantly changing course. But when caught, he's got plenty of bite with his mouthful of teeth to grind up the competition, especially anyone who hangs out around the Jersey shore, which is full of slimy beasts, especially ones who think they are tough, but they are no match for the Hadrotrumpus who is ready to bite and take them down.

Hadrotrumpus

FLYING REPTILES

The Trumpdactyl (aka the flying Pterodactyl with 3 foot wingspan that ate small insects and small animals and flew around North America, Europe, Australia, and Africa from the Jurassic to Cretaceous periods) is known for eating very small prey that get in its way. This way he is ready to swoop in to protect his domains, and he eagerly gobbles up any victims who don't quickly run away to live elsewhere or know how to hide or fight back when he swoops in for the kill or to scare his victims off of his lands.

Trumpodactyl

The Quetzalotrumpus (aka the 150 pound Quetzalcoatlus, the largest flying reptile with a 40 foot wingspan,who loved to feed on fish and scavenge dead kill throughout Texas during the Upper Cretaceous) was considered the most fearsome reptile by just about everyone. He struck fear into a growing number of victims, as he flew around more and more. Besides constantly prowling for new fish to fill his bill, like gathering cash in a cache, he knew how to gain even more as a super scavenger, who could turn anyone's kill into another tasty meal for himself, just like closing in and making a killing in a another huge deal.

Quetzalotrumpus

MARINE REPTILES

The Mosatrumpus (aka the 56 foot 15 ton Mosasaurus, who ate fish and other marine animals throughout Europe and North America in the Late Cretaceous) was the terror of the shallow seas. He was known for being sleek, fierce, and fast, so he could readily outrun almost anyone by leaps and bounds, until he suddenly found he over-estimated himself. So stronger competitors with more endurance caught up to him and took him down.

Mosatrumpus

The Pliotrumpus (aka the 12 foot 300 pound Pliosaur, who fed on fish and squid in the shallow seas of Europe during the Jurassic period and might even have survived as the Loch Ness Monster) is known for his elusiveness. First you see him; then you don't. First you think you know him; then you don't. That's how he's been able to survive for so long, since no one really knows who he really is. He may not even know himself, which is why he keeps changing what he says and thinks about this and that.

Pliotrumpus (maybe the Loch Ness Trump)

BIRDS

The Dodo Trump (aka the 3 foot tall 25 to 47 pounds Dodo Bird, who wandered around the Island of Mauritius feeding on nuts, seeds, bulbs, roots, and fruits from the beginning of the Paleocene to the mid-17th century) has found it hard going as has faced new predators and climate change and deforestation has destroyed his island retreat. But even so, he denies the climate is changing, and even if it is, he thinks he can control it or change it back. So that's why he is often considered a big dodo, and many new predators are gathering, so he won't be able to retreat much more.

Dodo Trump

The Great Trump Terror Bird (aka the 7 foot tall, 330 pound Giant Terror Bird, also known as the Titanis Walleri, who is a meat-eater and scavenger on the open savanna of Florida during the Pliocene) is the largest predatory bird that ever lived. He has the advantage of a huge beak which he can use like an ax to kill his prey, just as he can easily use his big mouth to kill an adversary with insulting and humiliating words. So now, anyone who crosses paths with the Giant Trump Terror Bird has to be careful, or this big bird will pounce and destroy, although more and more hunters are gathering together to shoot this bird so he will cease terrorizing everyone he confronts.

Giant Trump Terror Bird

MAMMALS

The Woolly Rhinotrump (aka the 12 foot 2 ton Woolly Rhino, who roamed around the Americas eating plants from the Pliocene to the end of the Pleistocene), is known for his short temper, like most rhinos. Challenge or confront him about anything, and he is quick to fume and snort in anger, so his challenger or opponent will quickly back down and go away. But when challengers stand firm, eventually he may back down, too, because the last thing he wants is an opponent exposing him by taking off his wool so he stands exposed to the world.

Woolly Rhinotrump

The Giant Trump Sloth (aka the 20 foot 4 ton Giant Ground Sloth or Megatherium, who ate plants through the Americas during the Pliocene to the end of the Pleistocene) is known for sometimes being slow moving and not overly bright, so he doesn't always stay up with the times and is especially dimwitted when it comes to knowing about anything outside of his usual stomping grounds. It's just foreign to him, so he doesn't think he has to know about it. And if he responds too quickly, he can easily fall into a trap. But once he is, he can be truly dangerous when cornered, since he can quickly strike back with the three huge claws on each front foot – much like a modern day devil, who is known for his cloven hoofs.

Giant Trump Sloth

The Saber Tooth Trump (aka the 4 foot 800 pound Saber Tooth Tiger or Smilodon who preyed upon all kinds of mammals, especially ground sloths and young mammoths in the Americas during the Pleistocene) is an especially vicious predator, who readily jumps on and takes on anyone who crosses him on his path. He is especially rapacious for females of any species, and he attacks young and old with equal abandon. And he often singles out minority members of the herd for his devastating attacks, though gradually, he has gone so far in his hunting that his prey have begun coming together to defend themselves and they have found ways to successfully attack him too. So his range is shrinking and shrinking, as predator becomes prey.

Saber Tooth Trump and Giant Cruz Sloth

The Mastotrump (aka the 9 foot 4 ton Mastodon, who roamed through the forests of North and Central America and fed primarily on the leaves and branches of conifer trees during the Pleistocene). He is especially known for traveling in herds, with most following blindly and others surrounding him like bodyguards, protecting him, because he has amassed so many foes as he raises his trunk and roars out insults at just about everyone who crosses his path – from Mexican immigrants and independent women to Muslims, Democrats, establishment Republican Party members, and media people who don't bellow the Trump party line. But if he isn't careful, he could find himself stuck in the La Brea tar pits if not the Madame Tussaud wax museum, where tourists come to laugh and gawk at how much like the wax figures are like the real ones, though sometimes the real figures look like wax, too.

Mastotrump

The Woolly Trumpoth (aka the 9 foot 2-3 ton Woolly Mammoth, a plant-eater who traveled in herds like modern elephants through Asia, Europe, Alaska, and Canada during the Pleistocene) has been gathering as large a herd as possible and is ready to trample anyone not in his herd. This way, with a big herd behind him, he roars loudly and tosses around his heavy trunk to scare off anyone who threatens to take any doubters out of his herd. Should they try, he stands ready to squash all comers with his very big foot. And he's always easy to find, because he leaves large footprints in his wake – and if things don't go his way, he's ready to roar even louder to anyone who will listen and gather his droppings.

Woolly Trumpoth

EARLY APES AND HUMANS

The Gigantotrumpus (aka the 9 foot tall, 1200 pound Gigantopithicus, who used to roam the bamboo forests of China, Vietnam, and Indonesia munching on bamboo, fruit and seeds during the Pleistocene) is known as the largest ape/primate to exist and is possibly the source of the Yeti and Bigfoot legends and sightings. But now he has been mainly sighted in the forests of Manhattan, jumping up and down and leaping on almost anything he can eat up, since he is so big he needs to consume a lot just to survive and thrive. Most recently, he has been extending his range around the globe, seeking to mow down everything in his path to become even bigger and greater, though he may have recently met his match that has been putting out his fire. So he may have to slink back to Manhattan, thinking about what else he can consume in the future.

Gigantotrumpus

Homo Trumilos (aka the 3 to 4.5 foot 70 pound Homo Habilis, who lived in Africa 2.8 to 1.5 million years ago during the Pleistocene and was the first stone tool maker and user) is known as an ape-like human who has mastered all kinds of tools. In fact, he not only sings the praises of his highly prized tool, but he loves tooling around in all kinds of ways – from riding in luxury cars and vans to super-fast sleek planes. Once known as "Handy Man," he now is called "Trump Man," because of the way he tries to trump everyone with his yells and trump calls, as well as with his army of guards who move around him and trump down anyone who gets too close.

Homo Trumpilis

Trumpo Erectus (aka the 4-6 foot 90-150 pound Homo Erectus, who roamed through Africa, the Mediterranean, and Western Asia from 1.9 million to 70,000 years ago during the Pleistocene; he was the first to use language, control fire, and migrate out of Africa). Unfortunately, his use of language has remained very coarse, and he is especially known for his grunts, yells, and short phrases used by little kids, such as "You're fired!" "That's huge!" and "Get 'em out of here." However, his ability to control fire has certainly evolved, as he has eagerly fired anyone and everyone, and he has developed an ability to get everyone fired up, so they are ready to attack his latest foe. He has also continue to migrate everywhere, as he has found places to put hotels, golf courses, and casinos all over the globe, though not all have stayed there, as a result of sinkholes and other eruptions, such as earthquakes and bankruptcies, that have taken them down.

Trumpo Erectus

The Neandertrump (aka Neanderthal, a 5 foot tall, 140 pound early human who lived and hunted throughout Africa and Eurasia 400,000 to 28,000 years ago in the Late Pleistocene. They made advanced stone tools, ornamental objects, and jewelry, built shelters, wore clothing from animal pelts, had a language, buried their dead, and lived in complex family groups.) And today, the Neandertrump does much the same, though he spends much more and makes everything much bigger than before, such as in the diamond and ruby necklaces and rings he buys from the most well-known jewelers. Plus, he buys expensive custom-tailored suits and gowns from the priciest stores, and he travels in luxury cars and private planes from territory to territory. He certainly has a very complex family group, too, with three wives and dozens of children and grandchildren from different wives. Plus, like his ancestors, he continues the tradition of keeping woman in their place to show them who's boss. And he loves to show off all his trophies, from his hotels and hundreds of branded items to his current trophy wife.

Neandertrump

The Homo Trumpien is a new subspecies of Homo Sapiens, who is known for his very aggressive, destructive nature. Sometimes called names by his opponents, like "narcissist," "sociopath," and "egomaniac," he easily ignores any insults or criticisms by claiming the opponent is dead wrong, while wishing he or she was simply dead. Unfortunately he often has grand plans that are really grandiose, or he revels in schemes to outdo his rivals, only to get undone himself when his plans unravel. So he is constantly overcoming one misfortune or dangerous escapade after another. Still he continues to rise and shine like the phoenix, only to be shot down again after another perilous flight that destroys others who come along for the ride. Even so, he is sure his next project will be "really great," "very huge," the "best of the best," or the most luxurious and lavish spread ever. But even as he builds more and more, he destroys more and more, too – so in a way, he has become the biggest and best destroyer ever. And, of course, his great extravagances and excesses, combined with his frequent braggadocio, have earned him the title of the biggest liar, too.

Homo Trumpien

The Homo Trumpus Trumpus is a newly developed subspecies of modern humans, who is especially known for his big head which contains his big ego. He commonly uses his short-stubby fingers to point out opponents who need to be silenced and removed from his presence. He is especially known for his ability to entertain, such as when he makes stupid and silly statements or plays dumb when asked questions he can't answer, such as about foreign policy. Additionally, he is known for his ability to be cunning and wily, like a fox, so he readily evades or hides from any question or person he doesn't like. And like a snake, scorpion, or other predator, he can quickly bite, sting, poison, or otherwise attack and seek to destroy those who oppose him. But if criticized for his action, it is never his fault – it is always someone else who started it; he is just going to finish it. Then, he goes on to give the next rousing speech or tweet to his supporters, who are ready to rush to his aid and attack his foes, like an army of red fire ants who spread their venom wherever they go.

Homo Trumpus Trumpus

And now for a look at modern human progress...

THE EVOLUTION OF HUMANS

New – Revised Based on the Latest News

Old – Based on Past Scientific Evidence

TRUMP IS NUTS!

An Illustrated Guide on the Many Ways that Trump Has Gone Nuts

INTRODUCTION

This book was inspired by the many discussions on Facebook and other social media sites by people who are appalled by Trump's rants and insults. Some created or shared cartoons that depicted Trump raging, and others shared or created names for Trump, such as Trumpelthinskin, Trump the Demented, Dingleberry Trump, Trumpty Dumpty, and more.

Many commenters even speculated that Trump was not merely a narcissist or sociopath, interested in only me, Me, ME!!!, humiliating anyone who opposed him, and winning whatever that took. But they also thought he was crazy, insane, and even suffering from early stage Alzheimer's.

Certainly, Trump's raging behavior and wild insults suggest a person who is out of control, unhinged, and literally nuts! And these ideas got me thinking about the many ways in which Trump might be nuts, using actual nuts to illustrate.

So in this spirit of wild and wacky fun, *Trump Is Nuts!* features a variety of nuts, along with nut cases and nuthouses, showing all the ways in which TRUMP might be considered NUTS! You might even grab some nuts and munch away, as you read this book and see Trump as many types of nuts.

A WHOLE LOT OF NUTS

When you get mixed nuts, you can't be sure of what you are getting, just that they will be mixed up. Likewise, the nuts who have joined with Trump are certainly a very mixed up lot, though they aren't very diverse. In fact, a lot of the nuts don't want to be mixed with others at all. They'd prefer to be in their own separate jar and hope others will want to buy that.

Mixed Nuts

Is Trump really a nut case? That's what more and more people believe, including some psychologists who have described him as having a "narcissistic personality disorder," whereby one thinks that everything is about me, me, me. Someone with this disorder also has delusions of grandeur about who one is and what one can do. Such a person can never be wrong and is ready to attack anyone who stands in his way, disagrees, or criticizes him. He always has to win whatever he does and makes excuses should he lose at anything, so he still comes out on top.

In other words, if you're not with Trump, you're against him and are fair game for insults, threats, and whatever else Trump can come up with to demean and humiliate you, whether in the media or in court. As such, he shares traits with other larger-than-life leaders like Hitler and Mussolini, to whom he is often compared, and some consider them nutcases, too.

It's a Nut Case

Being considered nuts can be difficult, because people want to group you with a lot of sick and crazy people who need to be put away or often get sacked from a job, because they seem to be out of control. Sacking them is a little like bagging wild animals – the rangers just have to catch them before they harm other animals or escape from their natural habitat to harm others. Likewise, a growing number of people, including Republicans, think that Trump is going insane and pulling them into a deep dark hole with him. So you might say they need to bag him or sack him by saying "You're fired," which is one of Trump's favorite lines, though when it refers to someone else.

A Bag of Nuts

POWER NUTS

As they say, cash is king, and so are cashew nuts. At least, if you've got the cash or caché, anyone can be king, or at least act like one. But once people lose their cash or caché, they're out of luck and just another nut. After all, once their royal accoutrements, such as a fancy robe, scepter, and crown are gone, people have little to set them apart from all the other mixed and mixed up nuts out there in the world, and they can easily get squashed.

In short, if you take the cash away from a cashew, what do you have left – just a great big EW!

Trumpking Cashew Nut

Almonds are everywhere – in cakes, cookies, and ice cream toppings. There is even an Almond Joy candy bar. But the Trump Almond Power Bar is in a class by itself, because it packs so much power. It'll give you more energy, assurance, and strength, so you can readily knock down, insult, and humiliate anyone you want – just like Trump does!

Trump Almond Power Bar

The Macadamia Nut is a round, hard shelled nut, which came to the U.S. from Australia by way of Hawaii. So it might be considered like a tough military nut, known for its strength and prowess – a tough nut to crack.

Yet, because it comes from elsewhere, it's not true blue American. So as an immigrant nut, maybe it should be deported, and never allowed to return to these shores, much less the supermarket shelves of America. As they say in the Marines – "Semper Fi!" And as they now say of this nut: "Bye, bye, Macadamia, goodbye."

Macadamia Nut (aka Military Nut)

The Trumpflower Seed is like a lowly Sunflower Seed, which became even tougher. So you might think of it like a warrior which attacks anything that might try to eat it up, such as birds flying by. In the process, it might even take down the American Eagle and all it represents – from the democratic courts to the laws of the land. The Trumpflower just has to spread enough of its seeds throughout the countryside, and soon there will be Trumpflowers everywhere. Thus, as the Trumpflower grows up big and strong, it will cover the land, so any plants that get in its way will soon wither and die. It all starts with a single seed that grows wild and crazy and out of control.

Trumpflower Seed

The Hickory Nut is definitely a super-powerful hard nut to crack. It is known for its hard, tough, nearly unbreakable shell, and the hickory tree with its often shaggy bark was perfect for making hickory sticks and switches, used to strike fear into anyone in danger of being hit. No wonder, at times, it became the rod of choice by jailers and schoolteachers for punishing anyone, when such punishments were legal.

If you've heard the expression, "spare the rod and spoil the child," most likely a hickory stick inspired those words of advice. Another popular expression, "Sticks and stones might break my bones," might be inspired by a hickory stick beating, too.

Now Trump would seem to be a great advocate for using this stick along with other methods of torture, including waterboarding, to bring any miscreants – or anyone who disagrees with him – to heel, and later to "heal." So as you can see, he's like a judge ready to dole out justice, which could be a good beating with a hickory stick from a hickory tree full of hickory nuts that could even double as stones should you want to stone anyone.

Hickory Nuts

TOUGH NUTS

The Wall-Nut, also popularly known as a Walnut, is great for creating walls, as well as in building all kinds of furniture, since it has a very strong, hard exterior that covers up its soft interior. Perhaps it's so strong on the outside to protect its inner insecurity. In fact, this inner nut is composed of two sections which look very much like the lobes of a human brain, where the left side is all about being rational, and the right side is all about being intuitive and emotional. If they are in balance, great. Otherwise – well, things can go boom in the night – or in the day, too. But the Wall-Nut can help, because it has long been used in gunstocks, as well as in cabinetwork. Plus the wall can be like the wall of a castle – keeping anyone and everyone out, while shooting now and asking questions later.

Wall-Nut

This pecan is a nut with old Southern roots, so no wonder it's proud of its old Southern traditions, from delicious pecan pies to KKK hoods, which are shaped much like the end of a pecan. Just poke in two holes and paint the pecan nut white, and voila, you've got a hood. In fact, since the pecan has a smooth, thin shell, it's perfect for heating up to make a pecan pie. But you don't want to stir it up too much, because then, due to its thin skin, it could easily explode and make a great big mess – in the kitchen or anywhere else, just like the KKK is making a big mess of things in the U.S. today.

Southern Pecan

Though the Cashew Nut is known for being one of the most popular nuts around, it is not really a real nut. Instead, it is a strange kidney-shaped seed that grows outside the bottom of a hanging fruit. Moreover, the cashew is only edible when roasted, so it is actually toxic at other times. In other words, it is a fraudulent nut that is called a nut because of its outer appearance. But then it could be very painful and difficult to impossible to digest, if it's not handled the right way. Even so, it might still claim to be a real nut, and others might claim this, too -- much like Trump and his followers often don't know what's true or real, and don't care.

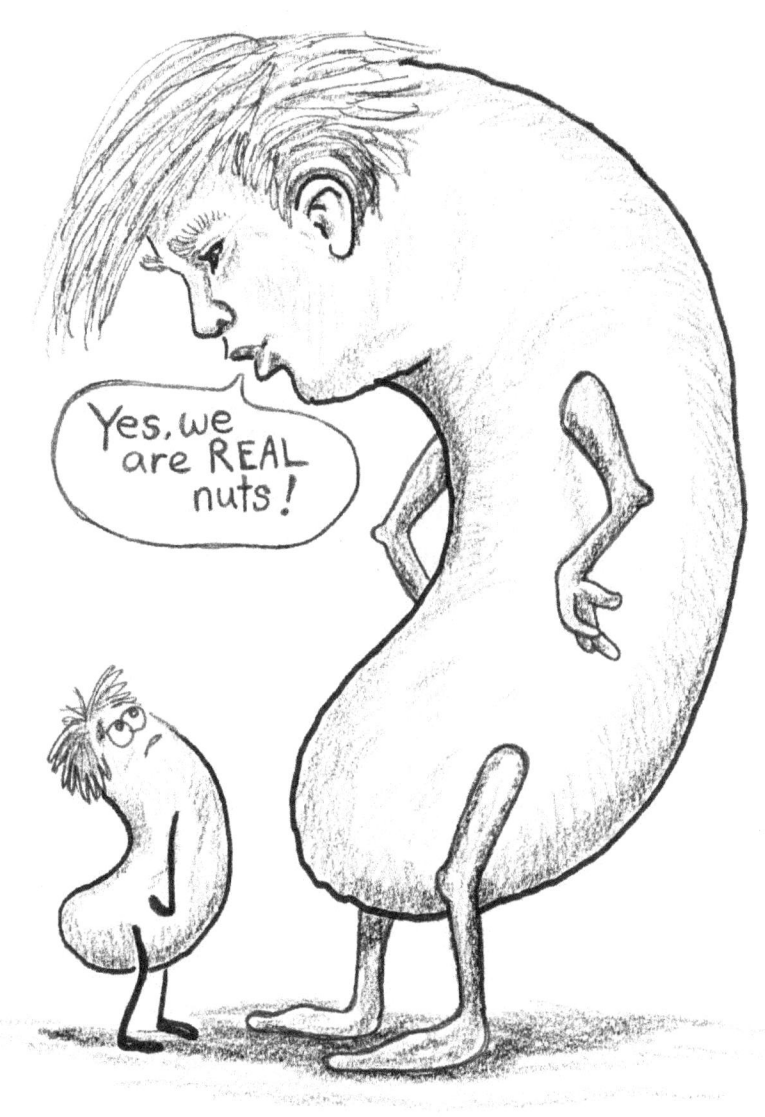

Just a Regular Cashew Nut

The Trumpkin Seed is one tough cookie…er seed, since it's not really a nut. Rather, it's a very strong seed, which comes from the pumpkin, a large, pulpy round fruit with a thick, orange-yellow rind that looks very much like Trump, who is sometimes called the Orange Man. Then again, with a few deep knife cuts, you have carved out the eyes, nose, and mouth to make a perfect Trump-O-Lantern for Halloween. Just have to put it in the window, and you can variously welcome or scare the neighbors, depending on whether you want to let them in or keep them out.

Still another characteristic of the Trumpkin Seed is that it's one of nature's testosterone boosters, which can quickly pump you up, so you can do well in a fight. Just pick out your enemies and start attacking them, thinking that testosterone boost will help you win. But all that testosterone can often make you testy, so if you pick the wrong fight with the wrong opponent, you might easily lose. Then in the end, they may say you've gone to seed, because you really weren't a tough nut after all.

Trumpkin Seed

MONEY NUTS

The Hazeltrump Nut, which comes from a variety of small shrubs or trees and has a smooth brown shell, has great bona fides as a native of North America and Europe, which is most known for its creamy spread. So it has been packaged as a great spread that you can put over anything. Or maybe use it to put over anything on anyone. It's especially good on bread – or for making bread through branding.

In fact, it's such a good spread, that you can put it in a jar and spread it everywhere and anywhere, which makes it an ideal surface spread. But look under the surface or try to get rid of it, and it can look a little like…well, you know, especially when you put globs of it together. Then, it can turn into a pile of…well, a Hazeltrump Nut paste, what did you think?

Hazeltrump Nut

Have you heard of a wingnut? Well, you will soon, because it will have the Trump Wingnut brand on it, just like Trump has branded steaks, vodka, casinos, health products, and a university. What's next? Why not wingnuts, since no one has thought to put a brand name on them. They are just put in a section of a shelf with all the other nuts, bolts, screws, and other hardware items. But now, with the Trump brand on wingnuts, hardware stores can announce these nuts are special and charge two or three times as much. The result is more money for everyone, unless of course, people decide to skip the Trump Wingnuts to get regular nuts, which are the same, but cost much less.

What's next if the wingnuts idea gets clipped? Maybe Trump screws. And why not? Trump is the expert in screwing up and screwing everyone.

Trump Wingnut Special

VERY NUTTY NUTS

Consider the Trump Coconut. Just like any coconut, it's got a hard shell outside, with lots of fuzzy barbs, so it looks like a head covered with frizzy hair. It's all white inside, like all good coconuts. Unfortunately, when coconuts fall out of trees in a tropical paradise, where many grow, they can crack open. That's how many coconuts get cracked, and when that happens, an army of ants can eat them up, just like an army of protesters can appear at the big Trump rallies and events. However, when attacked, uncracked coconuts can make great cannonballs to fire back – which is a good way to keep all that good white coconut meat inside.

The Trump Coconut

As its name suggests, the Brazil Nut hails from tropical South America, where it comes from a tree that bears hard, round, wood pods with about 20 to 30 nuts each. You might say this is like a community of nuts, where a group of nuts surround and protect all of the other nuts. However, if you get one nut alone, that could be very scary for it, because it could easily be eaten up. But before it is, it will fight like hell, and yell and scream to get away. But maybe it can't, and then it's goodbye Brazil. Still, you better not monkey around with this nut, because it's prone to throwing fits.

Brazil Trumpnut

Consider the Trump Pistachio Nut, which comes from the Mediterranean region and Western Asia, but mostly it's known for having an oily green kernel under its small hard shell. If you've ever had pistachio ice cream, you know it's unique for being very green. Well, that's just like Trump – very green because he is so new at trying to run for anything – from running for office to running the country, and being green, he doesn't know what he doesn't know.

Today, being green has become very popular, but there are all kinds of green, from greens on the golf course to the lush green of elegant lawns and having plenty of greenbacks or cash. And Trump is all of those, so the Trump Pistachio Nut fits him to a T for Trump – and it makes a great tea, too, which could be packaged and sold as one more Trump brand to buy and buy.

Pistachio Trumpnut

Sometimes people who act crazy are called "nutty as a fruitcake." They might also be called nutty as a "nutmeg," because this spice not only adds a spicy flavor in cooking, but in higher doses, it is used as an aphrodisiac and for its psychoactive effects. And the excessive use of nutmeg is definitely not recommended for people with psychiatric conditions, because it can make them go super nuts.

For example, if psychiatrists think someone has a narcissistic personality disorder, is a sociopath, or has delusions of grandeur or megalomania, they would not give that person any nutmeg. If they did, the person could go really cuckoo and tell their followers all kinds of crazy things about what they can do to get people to follow them. As a result, the nuts on nutmeg can have a very powerful effect with their mad ravings at big rallies, where their followers might think they are really GREAT rather than just GRATING. In fact, the Nutty Nutmeggers could even think they could shoot someone on a main street and their followers would still follow them – maybe even over a cliff. They just have to say whatever they want, and their followers will follow.

Nutty Nutmeg

A nuthouse is a perfect place for nuts, so as an alternative to the White House, some think that's a more suitable place for nut cases that are truly nuts. But it's up to the electorate to decide – though sometimes people who could belong in the nuthouse might end up in the White House and vice versa, since there's no qualifying nut test to determine if someone is certified to be President, such as being born in the United States. On the other hand, if one is properly certified, one can end up in the nuthouse. Or is the system nuts, because it isn't always possible to tell who's really nutty, and some of our policies are really nuts?

Welcome to the Nut House

NO MORE NUTS

As they say, from little acorns, big oaks grow. But that's only some of the time from this thick-walled nut that's usually set in a woody, cuplike base. Unfortunately, sometimes, mighty oaks can get off to a very bad start, such as if they get stepped on by a passing hiker or eaten up by a squirrel. Then, too, as the climate gets warmer and warmer, though some try to deny there is any climate change, a budding oak tree can shrivel up and die, because it is too hot and dry. It could even be consumed by a fire from lightning or a passing war. And sometimes small white worms can worm their way into these acorns. So instead of the beginnings of a strong, sturdy oak, out pops a small wiggly worm. Though you never know – Will it be an oak? Will it be a worm? Or will the acorn get squashed – so it will never become a mighty oak.

Fallen Acorn

Getting down to the nuts and bolts is like getting down to the brass tacks of something. Either way, you've got to know what you are doing, or you could end up with a screw loose. Or you might get a screwy idea, like a bolt from the blue, and then you could get really screwed. Thus, if Trump sometimes – or increasingly – seems to be losing it, perhaps that's why, which is why more and more people – from Democrats and independents to former Trumpkins, hope he mightt bolt away, like a horse bolting from a barn. However, in this case, no one regrets leaving the barn door open – they just hope the horse will run very far away and never come back. Usually people throw away the shells and enjoy the nut, but in this case, a growing number of people just want to throw away the nut.

Getting Down to the Nuts and Bolts

TRUMP IS AN ANIMAL!

An Illustrated Guide to the Way that Trump Fights Like Different Types of Animals

INTRODUCTION

TRUMP IS AN ANIMAL! was inspired by seeing the documentary *Life Story* on Netflix about the way animals of different species grow up, including the chimpanzee, tortoise, meerkat, and kangaroo. One commonality was that the males of different species frequently fight over power, females, and sometimes territory. After I previously created a series of books on Trump and the zany election, including *Trump Is Nuts!* and *Trump Is Extinct...or May Be Soon!*, I thought about the way Trump is constantly fighting everyone -- from other Republicans to Democrats, the media, homeowners in the path of his properties, and anyone else in his way. And if he isn't in the news for a few days, he'll say something outrageous and insulting to get the media and public to pay attention, while provoking those who are personally insulted or outraged by his remarks to argue back. So again and again, like many animals, Trump is ready to fight others for something he wants.

In the animal world, whoever is defeated typically withdraws and may even retreat from the group, and that often happens in encounters with Trump, though sometimes a defeated fighter will return with reinforcements to fight again, as do male chimps. But so far, Trump seems to keep winning most of the time, and he has amassed about 14 million voters who look up to him, because of his ability to fight the establishment, which is a source of their anger.

Thus, not only may Trump be nuts and going extinct sometime soon, he may fight like one of the animals featured in this book, as well as thousands of other animals. In fact, among most animals, there is so much fighting, especially among males for power, territory, and females, it is only possible to feature a small percentage of them.

Given this propensity to fight, TRUMP IS AN ANIMAL! features Trump as a variety of animals fighting other animals for power, territory, or females – and often for all three. After this, you may even see your dog or cat in a new way.

MAMMALS

Kangaroos are marsupials from Australia who have long been known for their prowess in fighting. They look like boxers in a ring and are built like fighting machines, with their powerful legs, tails, and upper bodies. They put up their paws much like a human boxer, and not only punch and jab with their front legs but use their tail and hind legs to punch their opponent everywhere and have large sharp claws on their hands and feet, which can do extensive damage to anyone who tries to attack them, much like Trump uses everything he's got to go after his adversaries. Kangaroos also have a thick stomach skin that protects them from serious injury, so they can quickly recover from one fight in order to fight again – much like Trump bounces from a fight with one group to another, and no matter how much any individual, group, or government official goes after him to insult him or report on his latest gaffes, he keeps coming back to fight some more. He's like the Engergizer Bunny – or in this case, the Energizer Kangaroo who keeps going…going…and going, his hands and feet poised to go still another round.

Most commonly, males fight with other males to determine who wins a particular female as a mate, though in Trump's case the battle is with other Republicans and Democrats for a particular office. Then, after winning over one female, the kangaroo looks for another female and the process begins again. The process might be a little like vetting a VP or deciding whether to do a deal with different business or trading partners. One sniffs around the person or company for a while, decides if it would be a good pairing, if so, does the deal and then moves on to the next.

Once a male kangaroo can show dominance, that can chase the other contenders away, much like Trump has scared away a series of Republicans in the Senate and House who have sought to challenge him and take away the nomination. So far, he has been able to fend them off, much like an aggressive male kangaroo is ready to fight off other males with his hands, feet, and tail, to reign supreme, like a boxer defending his title.

Kicking Kangaroos

Coyotes are known for being wily and tricky, and commonly win by intimidation. This way, they can threaten with their calls and cries, much like Trump. Described as "the most vocal of North American wild animals, they make at least 11 different kinds of sounds, which include woofs, growls, barks, yelps, and high-frequency whines, that are used for alarms or in challenging competitors. They also use howls to announce their presence.

Like a coyote, Trump is an especially tricky competitor, who may say one thing but do another, such as when he frequently changes his policies. Or he may lead someone to think he will get a certain position, but then he choose someone else, as Christie discovered, when Trump chose Mike Pence as his running mate, though his new choice held very different views than he did in many areas. But perhaps now he made his choice to appeal to his conservative supporters to maintain their support.

In any case, apart from confusing everyone, like a coyote quickly changing directions to lead pursuers astray, Trump is a master of attacking opponents with his angry words, barks, growls, and other sounds. If things don't go his way, he is continually howling and whining about something being unfair or the system being rigged, though he considers it fine if he is unfair to others. At still other times, he gives off a very loud long howl to announce his presence, as if to say, "You have to bow down to me and honor and obey whatever I say, because I am the king and I make the rules, whenever I want, but I can readily change my mind whenever I want, too."

Cunning Coyotes

Chimpanzees have always been fighters – just like Trump. Researchers of chimpanzee warfare have even found that lethal aggression is an evolutionary benefit, since the winners are rewarded with food, mates, and the opportunity to pass along their genes. Researchers have also found that bands of chimpanzees violently kill individuals from neighboring groups to expand their own territory, much like Trump may seek to overcome rivals to acquire new properties.

Chimps use all kinds of tools to fight with – from tree branches and sticks to clubs they find on the ground, whatever it takes to beat down an opponent and show who's boss. Though Trump uses documents, smart phones, and lawyers, the principle of using these modern tools is the same – do whatever you must to win, win, win!

Also, like chimps, Trump fights for everything – which has gotten him some great prizes, such as beautiful women as wives, mistresses, and lovers and real estate properties all over the world. However, as with chimps, not all fights are successful, so he has lost some properties, too. But he continues on to fight again another day, because being a winner is what's most important, no matter the fight.

Chimp Champion

Baboons, characterized by their long dog-like muzzles, heavy, powerful jaws with sharp canine teeth, and thick fur, are known for being very baaad -- especially the dominant males, who can be very nasty. They intimidate other males and others in the troop, as well as lurking predators outside the troop. They bite with their large canines to rip into anyone they take on, leaving death and destruction in their wake. They act like they are the kings of the open savannah, open woodland, and hills across Africa, as they eat almost everything as omnivorous predators and foragers. Baboons are also known for their loud vocal exchanges which help to establish and demonstrate their dominance.

Likewise, Trump, well-known for his furry hairpiece, likes to dominate and intimidate anyone he can, whether in his Republican Party troop or in the Democratic or other U.S. political parties. And he is ready to attack other countries, too, especially Mexico, China, and the countries in the Middle East, because he wants to keep out their people or undermine their currency. To do so, he claims he'll do whatever it takes, from waterboarding and killing the families of terrorists to getting better deals. Should you dare to oppose him, he's ready to attack, whether through nasty tweets, complaints to the media, or lawsuits for millions, which are like the loud vocal exchanges of the baboons. It is like baboons taking on all comers on the savannah or woodlands using any methods like can to get their way.

Baaad Ass Baboons

The African elephant is the largest living terrestrial animal. The males stand 10 to 13 feet tall and weigh 10,300 to 13,300 pounds. No wonder they have been chosen as the symbol of the Republican Party, and Trump has chosen this party to run on, because these elephants are very BIG and GREAT! After all, if he ran as a Democratic, even though at one time his policies were more in line with that party, such as favoring women's choice and LGTB rights, he would be stuck with a donkey symbol. And who wants to be a dumb beast of burden? Instead, in Africa, the elephant runs free and is the master of the savannah, because it is so GREAT!

Then, too, the elephant is a great symbol for Trump, because he loves circuses, and he has turned the Republican Party into a circus, with him as circus master, much like circuses have turned elephants and their masters into a featured attraction. These elephants have learned to perform a variety of tricks, much like Trump has treated the Party and the American people to all kind of tricks. He hasn't yet mastered a disappearing act, which about half the Republican Party and 70% of the American population would like. But he is GREAT at giving everyone a good show, turning usually boring politics into a continually entertaining and humorous event for the past year. And maybe he'll continue to be a great act over the coming months or even years, until the final curtain, which could be curtains for the U.S., too. But everyone is having lots of fun, right?

As for fighting, usually over females for mating, bull elephants first try intimidation to scare rivals away, but fight if they are more evenly matched. Though elephants rarely kill other elephants, they seriously injure each other, and the loser runs away to avoid a pair of tusks in the backside, much like Trump's rivals have lost and have quickly run away.

Trump Elephants

Hippos are huuuge. Though they are mostly herbivores, they are anything but peaceful vegetarians, since they are highly aggressive and unpredictable and are considered among the most dangerous animals in Africa. As such, they are much like Trump, who responds largely from his intuition and whim, and is ever ready to attack anyone for anything deemed insulting or offensive to him . And he likes everything to be "huuge," "great," or otherwise "extraordinary."

While hippos may look a bit like pigs, they are most closely related to whales and porpoises and spend much of the time immersed in rivers, lakes, and mangrove swamps. There, the bull collects a harem of 5 to 30 females and their young, and he keeps cool by staying in the water or mud, a little like a modern-day corporate chief might relax in a pool with a group of women and young assistants, who cater to his every need.

Besides being huuge, hippos are especially known for their huge jaws. Apart from eating, the males spend much of their times fighting with other males, and when they fight with their big mouths wide open, they use their large teeth to block each other's attacks or inflict injuries. The display of their huge open mouths is a little like Trump's attacks with his big mouth, which he uses to insult and humiliate revivals and defend against any attacks with an even bigger attack to fight back.

Another Trump-like characteristic is the way the hippos mark their territory by defecation. In other words, they spread lots of shit around to keep other hippos away – and according to some rivals and media folks, Trump sure does much the same since about 91% of what he says is lies – in other words, it's full of shit!

Huuuge Hippos

Rhinos are characterized by their large size, since all species reach a ton or more in weight, and they have a thick protective skin. However, they have relatively small brains for mammals of this size – only about 400-600 grams, as well as a large horn, which humans will kill for.

This small brain means rhinos are not very bright, much like Trump according to many political commentators, because he doesn't know much about things that most politicians know about, such as the Constitution or names of some countries. But then, like a rhino, he can push away the questions that probing journalists ask about his seeming lack of knowledge or misstatements, because of his outer thick skin. Even so, he doesn't take criticism very well and often responds by going ballistic with a flurry of Tweets, because underneath that outer armor, he seems to have a very thin skin.

In any event, once a rhino decides to take on another rhino, usually to show dominance and win over females, he first tries intimidation. He stares the other male down in hopes he will retreat. But if that doesn't work, a nasty shoving and butting match follows, which can end with the loser gored by the winning rhino's big horn.

Unfortunately, that horn can be a prized possession for humans, so they may hunt rhinos to kill them and take their horns, much like the Democrats and anti-Trump Republicans have been trying to take Trump down to get his mojo, or horn, so to speak. Their hunting cry is "Dump Trump" or "Never Trump," and they want him out of the race. But he seems to be successfully goring both the Democrats and Republicans out to get him. Even so, they keep coming back for more, so the fight for the Presidency has turned into a truly gory battle, though no one is sure yet about whose ox …er…rhino has been gored the most.

Republican Rhinos

The Trump Cape Buffalo, or Trumpalo for short, is the most dangerous animal in Africa, besides hippos and crocodiles. While they do their killing and fighting in the water, the Trumpalo fights on land or about the land. Though the Cape Buffalo is not very tall – only 4 to 5 feet high with short legs, it is massive. It weighs about 1000 to 2000 pounds, and the bulls have especially thick and wide horns. So you might say they are known for throwing their weight around, much like Trump, whether he's negotiating land deals or taking over the Republican Party and changing the political universe forever. How? With his bullying tactics, he buffalos his way around wherever he is to get what he wants.

You can never predict exactly what the Cape Buffalo will do, so unlike its closest buffalo relatives in Asia, the Cape Buffalo has never been domesticated, due to this unpredictable nature, which makes it very dangerous to be around. Likewise, Trump is known for his unpredictable nature, where he quickly shoots from the hip and changes his policies and positions almost on a whim, based on what he thinks others want to hear – or what he thinks they should hear.

Unfortunately, one of the Cape Buffalo's major weaknesses is being subject to foot-and-mouth disease, an infectious and sometimes fatal viral disease which causes a high fever for two to six days, followed by blisters inside the mouth and on the feet that can rupture and result in lameness. And likewise, Trump certainly shows some signs of this disease, when he puts his foot in his mouth on many occasions, which could prove fatal to his candidacy, though always he seems to recover, until he puts his foot in mouth again.

So like the Cape Buffalo, will Trump stomp and dominate his way to power? Or will he end up as a big celebrity trophy, just as the Cape Buffalo is a member of the big five game animals who are a sought after trophy in hunting?

Trumpalos

The Trumphorn Sheep, also known as the Bighorn Sheep, might be considered one more Trump brand, along with Trumps Steaks and Trumps Vodka, which went belly up. It is a native of North America and is known for its big horns, which can weigh up to 30 pounds, while the sheep can weigh up to 300 pounds. The Bighorns from the Rockies are especially large, with some males over 500 pounds. So these sheep are good at throwing their weight around, just like Trump, and they have extra thick skulls and neck vertebrae, so they can better absorb the impact of clashes with others and quickly recover to fight again.

Like Trump, these sheep like living in high places. While they live on alpine meadows, grassy mountain slopes, and the foothills near rugged, rocky cliffs and bluffs, Trump similarly lives on high in the towers of Manhattan. In turn, both are well adapted to climbing the steep terrain, which helps to provide a cover from predators. For example, when threatened by potential enemies, like the members of a lawsuit against Trump University, Trump can readily seek cover in the steep terrain, like the Bighorn Sheep, such as by retreating to his luxurious penthouse, high atop a Manhattan skyscraper.

Unfortunately, a potential hazard of living in steep, rugged terrain is getting hit by a rock or falling off a cliff, as has happened to some sheep, and sometimes this has happened to Trump, such as when he has filed for bankruptcy four times. But he has the agility to get back on his feet and climb back up to the heights again.

This heavy weight and agility also comes in handy when the sheep fight to establish a dominance hierarchy before the mating season, and fight like boxers in a ring. The two competitors first walk away from each other, then turn to face each other, followed by jumping and lunging at each other with head butts and clashing horns, until the biggest headbanger wins. You might say that Trump similarly butts heads with many different people, and most of the time, he manages to win and climb to higher and higher heights.

Trumphorn Sheep

Elk, one of the largest species of deer and one of the largest land mammals in North American and Eastern Asia, are known for their large antlers which the male elk shed each year. They live in or near the forest, where they eat a variety of grasses, plants, leaves, and barks; and during the mating season, the males show off what they can do. It's like an elk reality show, where they vie to be at the top of their game to win the grand prize – mating with the most desirable females of the herd.

Among other things, while seeking to establish their dominance among other males, the male elk posture, wrestle with their antlers, and engage in bugling, where they loudly make sounds like a bugle, that can be heard for miles. As they fight, the loud sounds attract females who want to mate with the winner, much like Trump may yell out words at a rally or ramble on about a current topic and talk about how great he is, and how he has been right about this and that. Then, too, Trump might bugle in the way he repeatedly calls out insults to take down one rival or another, such as calling out "Liar…Liar…Liar," to refer to Hillary, even though the media shows he lies much more. In turn, any rival or media person subject to the Trump treatment, might say they have been "bugled," called out like an Elk seeking to show he is the most powerful, dominant, and GREATEST Elk of them all.

Intriguingly, the elk is much like Trump in one other way in that some cultures revere the elk as a spiritual force, while in some parts of Asia, antlers are used in traditional medicines to heal. Likewise, Trump might like to think of himself as a spiritual force -- like a god to be worshiped and revered like the Elk. Then, too, he seems to think he can heal the planet, such as by declaring war on ISIS and getting the countries in the Middle East to provide the troops, much like he calls for building a wall to keep out Mexican immigrants and expects Mexico to pay for it. But then, as an all-powerful god, he might think he only has to issue a command and it will be done, on earth like it is in Heaven. Just ask and he will receive, like the entitled god that he is.

Trump Elk

While male bears typically fight other male bears for the usual reasons – to show who's the dominant male, subdue other males into submission, and get females to mate with – they sometimes fight female bears who are trying to protect their cubs from attack. Then, they bite and claw at each other, much like Trump has sought to fight Hillary to the death, while the Democratic Party is like her cubs. And just like the male bear might use all types of tactics to destroy the female to get to her cubs, so has Trump ferociously gone after Hillary.

At one time, he sought to charm and disarm her as a businessman seeking benefits from a powerful figure in government, when Hillary was first lady. But now he seems ready to do anything to defeat her and destroy her cubs, from calling her "Crooked Hillary" to repeatedly calling her out on her emails, so that her mistakes might lead to her destruction, just like a male bear might repeatedly attack a female bear to make her grow weak in order to destroy her and her cubs. Then, once the female is defeated, he could again show the other bears that he is the biggest, most powerful of them all, like a Bearzilla, who can't be beat.

Battling Bears

Male lions are like constant fighting machines, starting from when they are young males and the older males kick them out from the pride, which includes one dominant male, his females, and their young. Once forced out, the young males have to roam around to find another pride of lions, so they have to fight with the resident male, often to the death, and sometimes they call on their buddy lions to help them. Once they win, they kill all of the cubs, so they won't be stuck with another lion's cubs.

The process is a little like Trump taking down other Republican candidates or anyone else who stands up against him, from Senators to members of the media. He pushes them out, so he can reign supreme like a head lion.

The lion's distinctive mane is a sign of his power – the darker and fuller the mane, the healthier the lion, and lionesses tend to favor males with the densest darkest manes. In turn, the testosterone hormone is linked to mane growth, so having a huge full mane might be considered a sign of masculinity, much like Trump likes to show off his huge head of blond hair. It's a toupee, but no matter – the flowing gold locks suggest virility and power, much like the lion's mane.

Unfortunately, just as lions can gain power over a pride by fighting, so they can lose it when a stronger lion comes along, such as if a Hillary Clinton, Bernie Sanders, or if a coup by Republican Party members takes him out. Then, since lions commonly fight to the death and the loser gets exiled, that might be the outcome for Trump -- the death of his political hopes, and maybe exile to the golf courses around the world, where Trump might go to live out his senior years – no longer as an all-powerful lion; just another loser like a no-longer dominant lion, though he might still win on the course.

A Losing Lion

Like Trump, Fur Seals like to show they are heavy weights, much as male lions do on the savannah, since they are like the lions of the seals, since they are more closely related to sea lions than true seals. They are especially known from their dense underfur, and they enjoy hanging out in colonies on the beaches, where the dominant males mate with more than one female – much like Trump can boast of having three wives, along with numerous mistresses and short term relationships with beautiful women.

But while male Fur Seals can have lots of females for themselves, they aggressively choose and defend the females in their harems from other males, because only the dominant male gets the females – though only as long as he remains dominant. The result is big fights as the males battle each other, until the dominant male either maintains his place, or if the usurper wins, he essentially loses everything. Then, he often slinks off to sea, since he has lost his place in the community.

That fight between the male seals is a little like what has gone on in the political arena. First, Trump fought off all of the challengers in the Republican Party to become the nominee. Next, he has repelled a series of challenges to take away his Republican Party harem by the #NeverTrump movement and others telling the delegates to vote their conscience, which would mean voting for someone else. And then, he has still more challenges from Hillary and the Democratic Party before he can take the final prize – the Presidency. And if he doesn't win, well, maybe he'll have to slink off, too. Though instead of going off to sea and disappearing like a male Fur Seal who has lost his place, he may just go off and play golf and do more business deals, since he is out of the political game, but still has other games which he can play.

Trump Fur Seal of Approval

Meerkats are known for being especially feisty and aggressive, just 4like Trump, despite their very small size, since they are only about 12 inches tall. They live all over the Kalahari Desert in Botswana, and a group of them are called a mob, gang, or clan, much like some casino owners in Las Vegas have been part of such a group. And at one time, Trump was a casino owner before the Trump Casino went bust, so he might have mob, gang, or clan ties, too. These meerkat groups commonly include about 20 meerkats, though some super-families have 50 or more.

Meerkats are especially known for the way the group organizes to go out looking for food and avoid predators. A sentry stands guard, watching out for predators, such as eagles and jackals, while other meerkats go look for food. Their system is a little like the way Trump has a team of bodyguards to watch over him while he goes to large rallies seeking support from potential voters. But should some protesters appear, the bodyguards will jump into action, much like the sentry meerkat will suddenly cry out to warn the others. They use different cries to indicate the seriousness of the danger -- from low to medium to high urgency, as well its source – whether it's an aerial predator like an eagle or a terrestrial predator like a jackal or snake. Then, the foraging meerkats will rush away to head home to the safety of their burrow, much like what happens when things turn violent at a rally because of the protesters. Then, the police will rush in, and in some cases, Trump's bodyguards will lead him to a car and drive him away.

Like most other male animals, meerkat males are ready to fight as needed with others within their group. Commonly, a male will fight with other males to establish dominance, and will fight with a female who resists him until she submits. Subsequently, the dominant male and female pair may kill off any other offspring not their own, and they may evict or kick out the offsprings' mothers, who will often join a group of males to form a new meerkat group. In this way, meerkats keep their power all in the family, much like Trump has brought in his family members to run his businesses and help run his campaign. This way he can better be sure of everyone's loyalty and maintain his power.

Mighty Meerkats

BIRDS

Roosters, also known as cocks, normally fight other roosters for dominance, power, and mating rights, expressed such terms as "rule of the roost" and terms like "cocky," "cocksure," and "cock of the walk." But the losers still live to fight another day. By contrast, in cockfighting, two roosters bred for aggression are placed beak to beak in a small area so they will fightto the death, while fans cheer for their bird to win.

It's a fight with a long history, since the sport of cockfighting goes back 6000 years. Modern cockfighting was first documented in 1521 when Magellan sailed to the Philippines and the earliest known book about it was published in 1607 as *The Commendation of Cocks and Cockfighting."* The rooster's ability to fight is often increased by putting sharp knives or dagger-like attachments to break bones or to pierce an eye or lung to inflict maximum damage. The winner is the bird who inflicts the most damage or kills the other bird first, though later, one or both birds can die because of the severity of their injuries.

Trump's battle to winning the Republican nomination and then inflicting as much damage as he can on Hillary is much like that. Though none of the other Republican contenders were actually killed, some emerged from the battle so damaged that they may never run again or will be likely to lose when they have other political fights. And now that he is fighting Hillary, Trump is using any weapons he can – from her email scandal from using a private email server for government business to earlier problems like Whitewater and Benghazi to call her "crooked" Hillary. Meanwhile, his other battles, like about 4000 lawsuits, four bankruptcies, two divorces, and a recent claim of rape, might be viewed like preliminary bouts getting him ready for the main event – the run for the Presidency – while the American public following the saga on the news and social media, might be compared to the spectators watching cocks battle it out in a ring.

So may the games continue and may the best cock…er candidate…win.

Cock Fighting

As in most species, male penguins fight to compete for a possible partner or a good nesting place. Sometimes a male may fight another male who has paired up with his own partner, just like a jealous husband might attack a male who he discovers is having an affair with his wife.

When a fight breaks out, penguins typically fight with their wings and beaks, though before then, a penguin may threaten another male to go away, such as by using an intense threatening stare, or combining a stare with pointing their bill towards their opponent. Then, once an opponent comes into range, both will fight with their bills and squeeze their eyes half-closed to protect them. Alternatively, if a penguin goes on to attack, it will lean forward, extend its wings and open its bill, while it rushes forward to attack. You might compare these battle moves to an attack or defense by Trump, except instead of wings and his beak, he flails his arm and short stubby fingers around, and he hurls insults from his mouth.

Or sometimes, like a penguin, Trump may engage in a stealth attack to take away someone's money in a deal or steal their votes. While the penguin may steal the pebbles another male penguin collects to show his power, for Trump, this theft can take various forms, from cheating employees out of their full wages to hiding money from the tax collector to using eminent domain to take houses away from older residents who don't want to move so he can build a hotel or club on the land. However he does it, like a male penguin, Trump ends up gathering and hording up as many objects of wealth as he can. It's all part of the deal of getting as much as you can to show off your power, and if you make another competitor mad, so much the better. You are a king, much like a king of the King Penguins. And being king you can show off your wealth and claim you are better than anyone else, until of course you lose your money or your pebbles.

Penguin Power

As large, powerful birds of prey, with a heavy head and beak, eagles go after what they want and get it. Most eagles are even larger than any other raptors, apart from some vultures, so if pitted against a vulture, say like Trump, they could probably take him down.

Like all birds of prey, eagles have a very large hooked beak to readily rip flesh from their prey, and they have strong muscular legs, powerful talons, and very keen eyesight. So once they have their eyes on a likely target, that target could well be toast.

Intriguingly, in contrast to most species, the female eagle is larger than the male, and when female eagles lay two eggs, the older, larger chick frequently kills its younger sibling once it has hatched. In turn, this dominant chick tends to be a female, since they are bigger than males, and the parents don't do anything to stop the killing. In other words, among eagles, females rule!

This seems like a fitting parallel today, since the bald eagle is America's national bird, and in a fight with a female, the male is bound to lose – much like Trump might be ripped apart by Hillary – a fitting end to a long battle. Or then, again, maybe the American eagle might go in for the kill, so it can soar high once again and prevail in these dangerous times that have unleashed frightening forces and people upon the world.

Eagle Power

REPTILES

Galapagos tortoises, which only exist on two remote archipelagos – the Galapagos Islands near Ecuador and Aldabra in the Indian Ocean near Tanzania, are known for being very huuuge, since they are the largest living species of tortoise. They can grow up to six feet and weigh up to 900 pounds. They also have a very hard shell and short neck, much like Trump has a short neck and claims to have a thick skin. But while he might retreat to his Trump Tower in Manhattan which is like a large protective shell, he seems to have a thin skin underneath his outer shell of wealth and property. That's why he responds with rage like an angry tortoise ready to attack as soon as anyone says anything he considers a put down, like saying he has less money than he claims he has.

Male tortoises also engage in aggressive behavior with each other to win the right to mate with any available females, and their fights can include biting and last for many hours before one leaves in defeat. Likewise, once Trump is determined to fight a rival or support a position, the fight can go on for a very long time, such as when he repeatedly claimed that Judge Gonzalo Curiel was biased against him, because he said he wanted to build a wall and get Mexico to pay for it – and Curiel was of Mexican ancestry.

Finally, Trump is like a tortoise in that tortoises are very slow moving, so some think of them as lazy creatures, since they move at a very slow and leisurely pace to keep their body temperature down, due to having a very slow metabolism. Likewise, some describe Trump as being lazy, since he seems to have little interest in learning about government policies and practices. Rather, he likes to shoot from the hip, say whatever he thinks at the moment, and doesn't want to take the time to learn any of the details. The approach might contribute to his being more efficient in the use of energy, much like the slowing moving tortoise needs to use less energy. But the downside is that Trump often gets his information wrong or wants to change his mind after making a choice, such as when he had second thoughts about who to select for his VP, though he decided to go with his initial choice after all.

Trump the Tortoise

The Komodo Dragon is another very huuuge beast. It is the largest living species of lizard and is found on a half-dozen Indonesian islands, where it can grow up to 10 feet and weigh up to 150 pounds. Why so large? Because these dragons are believed to be part of a relict population of large lizards that died out during the Pleistocene, but they survived. So now because of their large size, they essentially rule the roost where they live, and they successfully hunt and ambush all kinds of prey. Likewise, Trump at 70 might be viewed as something of a relic who is continually fighting to show he is still strong and powerful, though he uses various supports to show his power, such as bodyguards to provide a wall of protection when he speaks at a rally, and he has a team of lawyers ready to file lawsuits should someone defame or besmirch his name or his properties.

The Komodo Dragons are similarly great fighters, and one of the tools in their arsenal is their venomous bite, which might be compared to the venom that Trump often spits out. The Dragons do most of their fighting between May and August during mating season, when the males aggressively fight over females and territory. They grapple with one another on their hind legs, and eventually, the winner pins the loser to the ground. Then, the winner will flick his long tongue at the female to check if she is receptive. Though females typically resist at first, the male has to continue to be strong, since he must fully restrain the female in order to mate. Likewise, Trump is ready to attack and hold down anyone who resists his effort to get what he wants.

Dueling Dragons

The Anaconda, a relative of the python, is the largest snake from tropical South America. It can grow to more than 29 feet, weigh more than 550 pounds, and measure more than 12 inches in diameter. It is one of a minority of animals where females are larger than males.

These snakes eat each other and anything else they can ambush, including pigs, deer, jaguars, birds, turtles, and caimans. A snake constricts its prey by squeezing until its victim is asphyxiated. Then, with its large jaws, it swallows its prey whole and digests it at its leisure for the next weeks or months.

Likewise, Trump, who is often called a snake by his detractors, can easily squeeze the life from his competitors, political rivals, and underpaid workers at his hotels and golf courses. Whatever the reason, as he puts on his squeeze by not paying, paying less than due, saying damaging words, or filing suit, the victim commonly succumbs. Though sometimes there's a rare exception, such as when the media reports on a victim's story and a public shaming leads to his occasional retreat.

On the other hand, since the female is larger than the male, a male Anaconda needs to beware the female attacker, because he could end up being squeezed to death himself, much as might occur as Hillary revs up her attacks on Trump and goes in for the kill.

Snake Eyes

PART IV: POEMS

DEAR DONALD TRUMP, WHAT'S WRONG WITH THE FBI?

Dear Donald Trump, What's Wrong with the FBI?
A. Concerned Citizen

Were they getting too close in finding the spies?

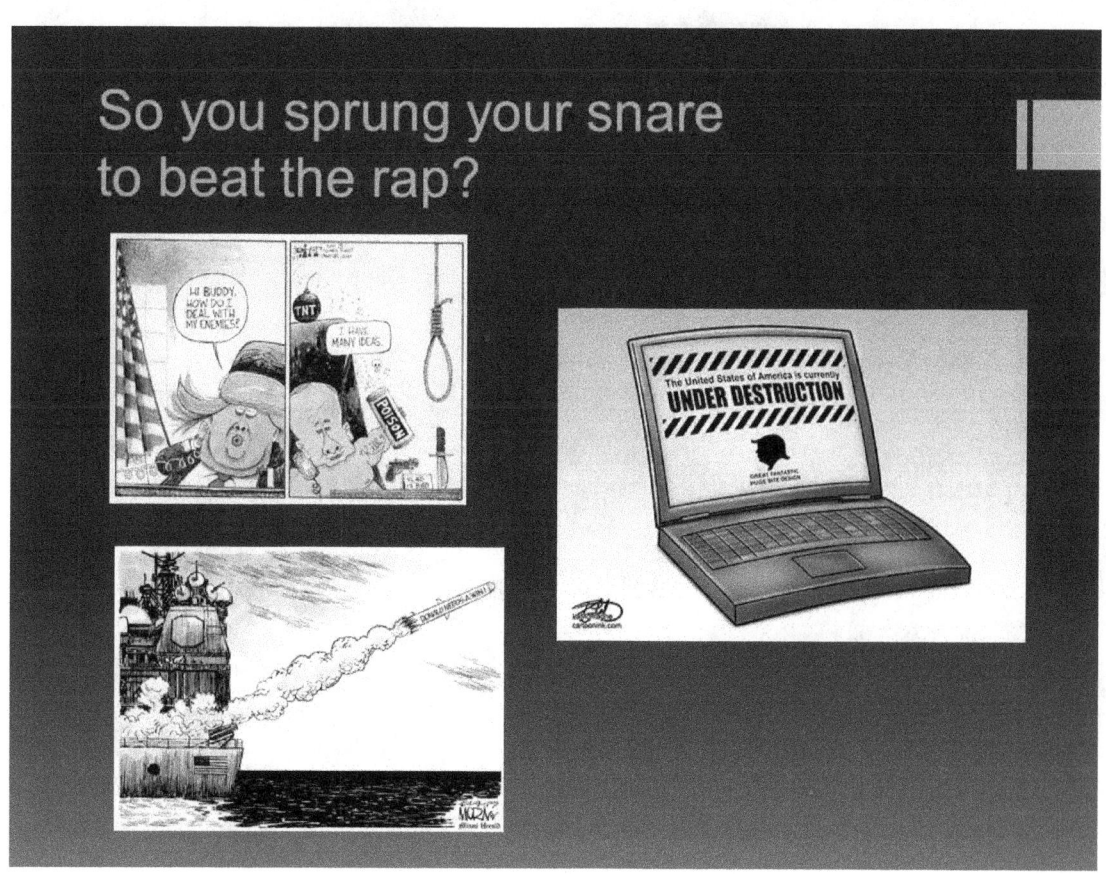

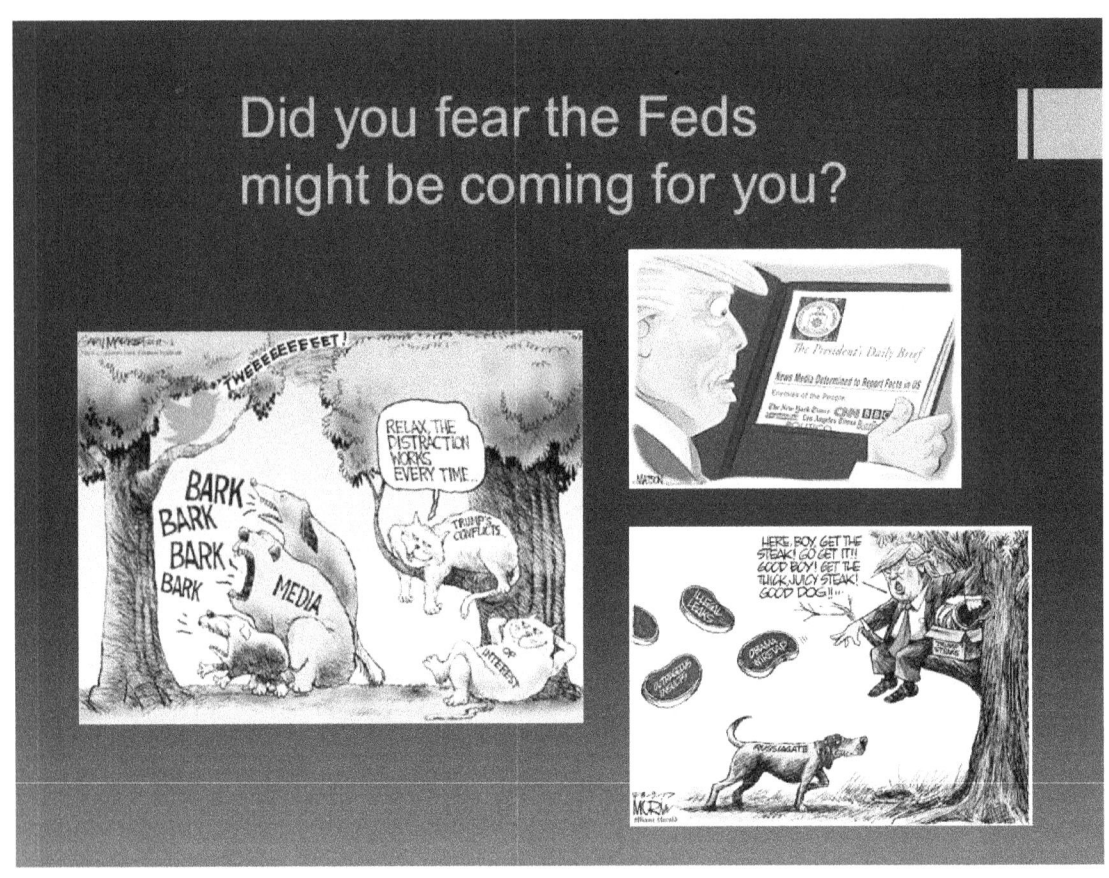

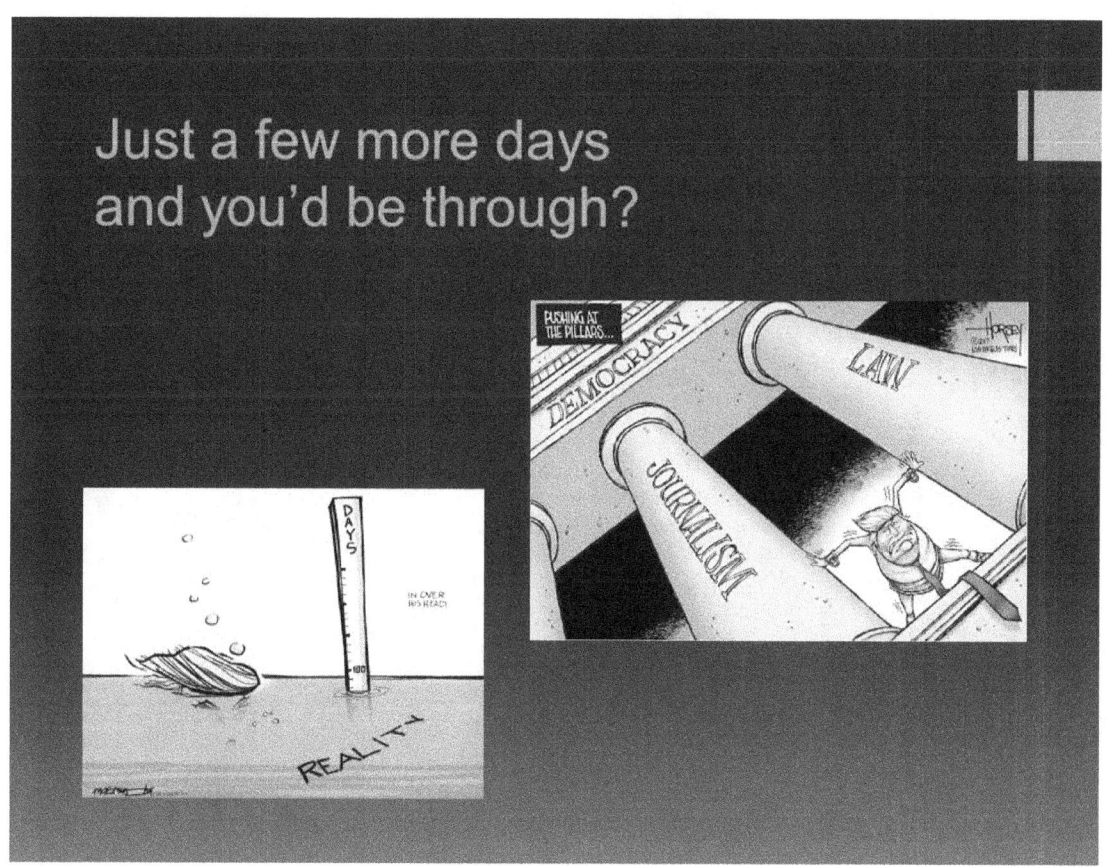

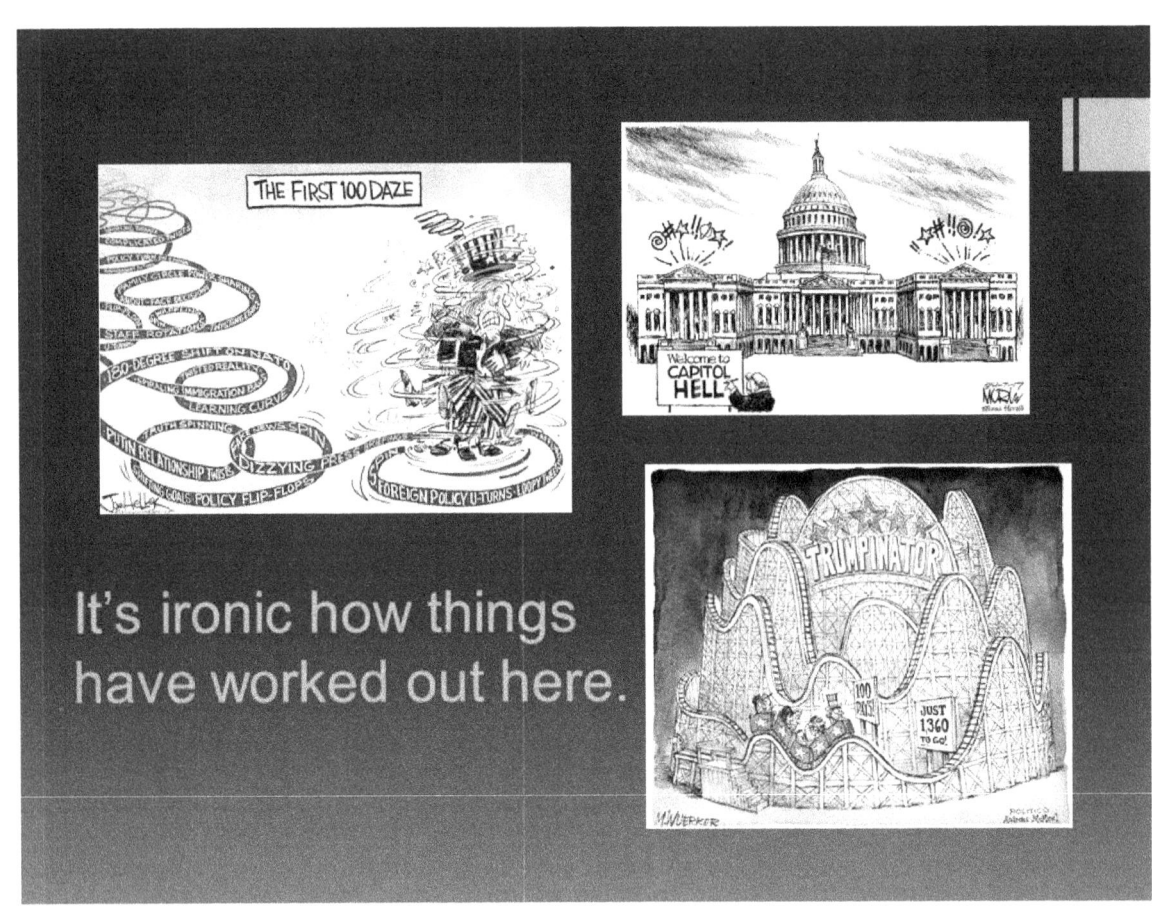

Yet that's karma: getting Hillary out, so you got in.

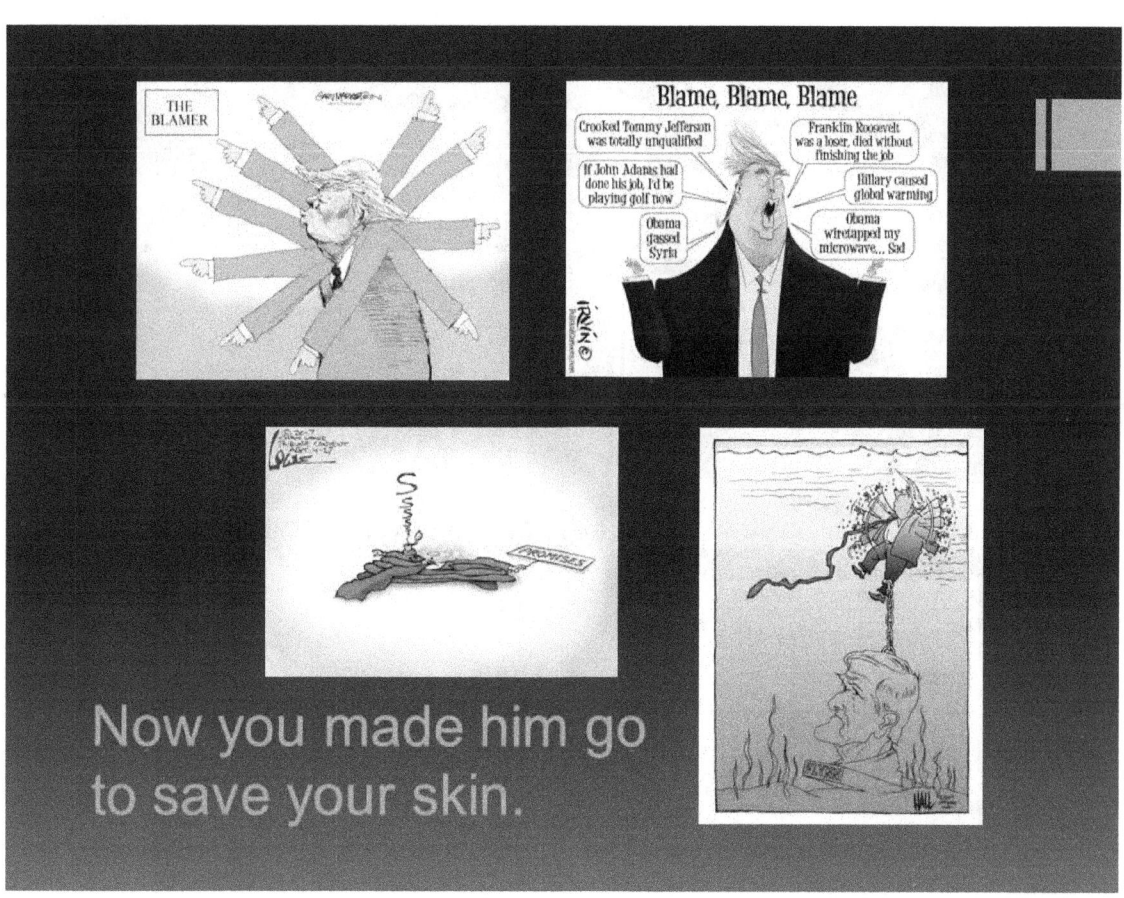

Now you made him go to save your skin.

You spun a great D.C. thriller
Now it's time for the final twister!

The End… Let's Hope!

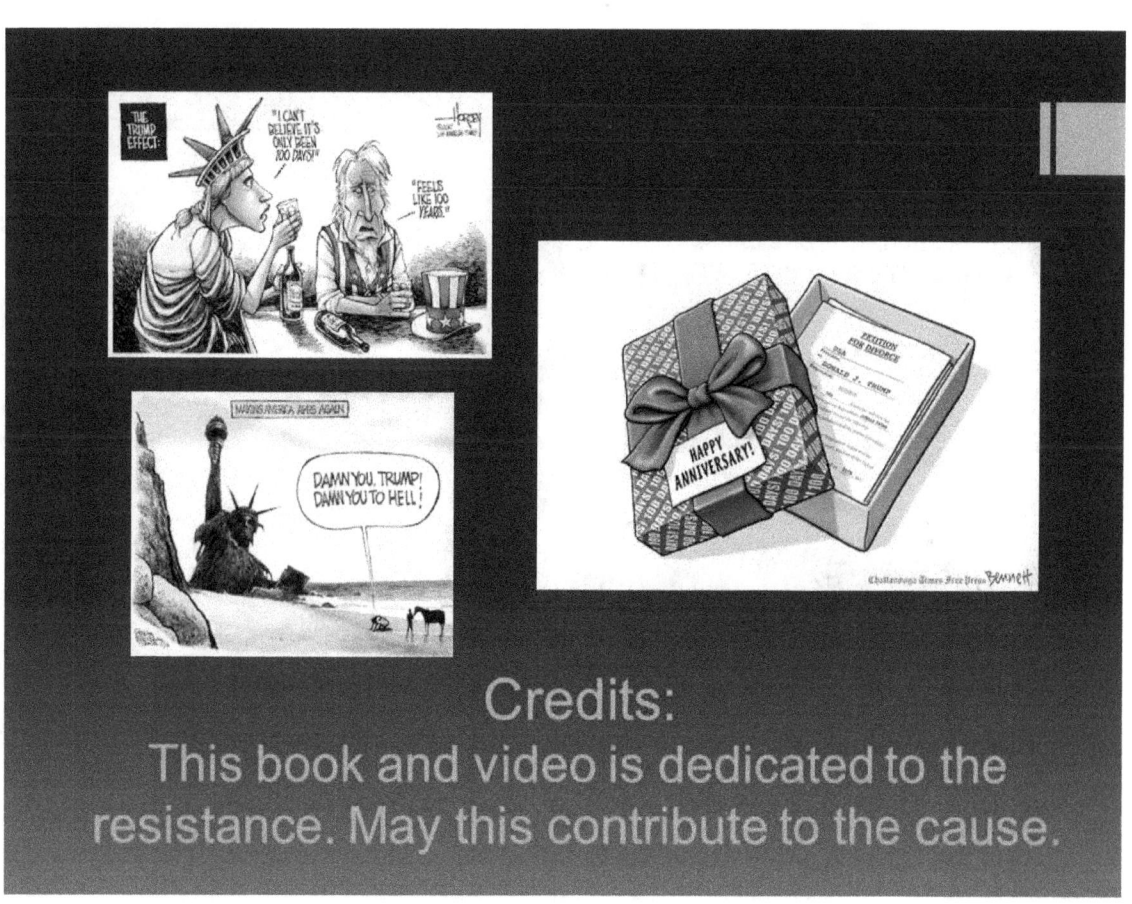

Credits:
This book and video is dedicated to the resistance. May this contribute to the cause.

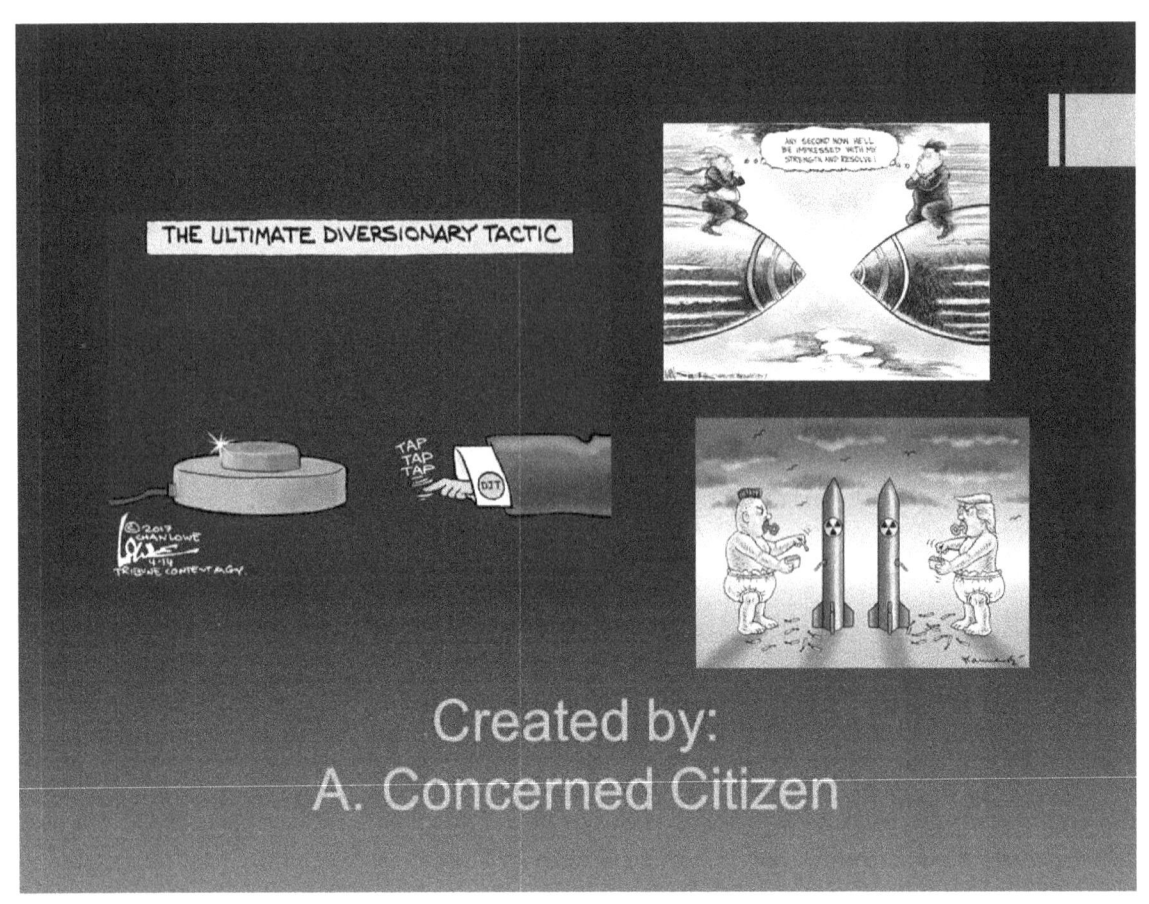

And thanks to the many photographers and cartoonists whose photos and cartoonists inspired the resistance.

DEAR DONALD TRUMP, ARE WE GOING TO WAR?

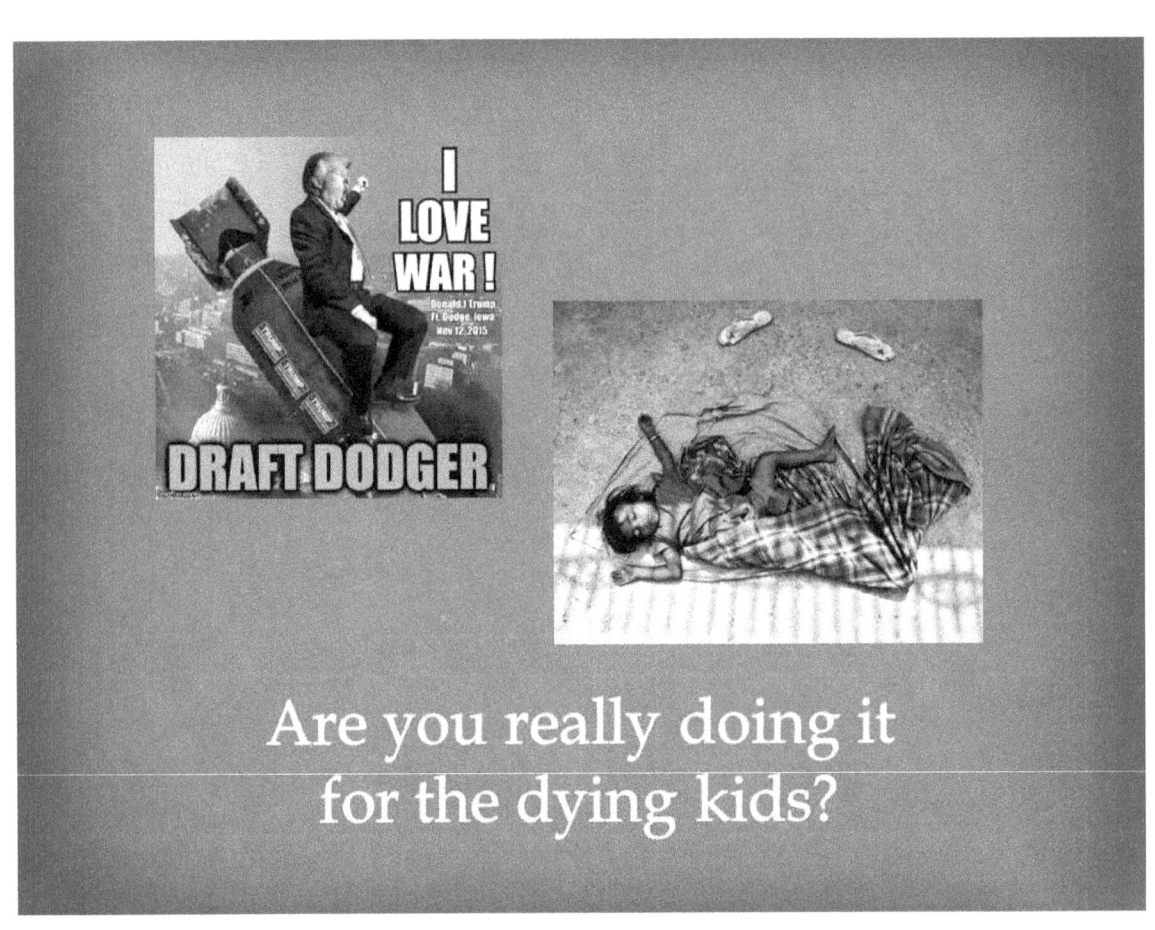

Or are the bombs
and flames all for show?

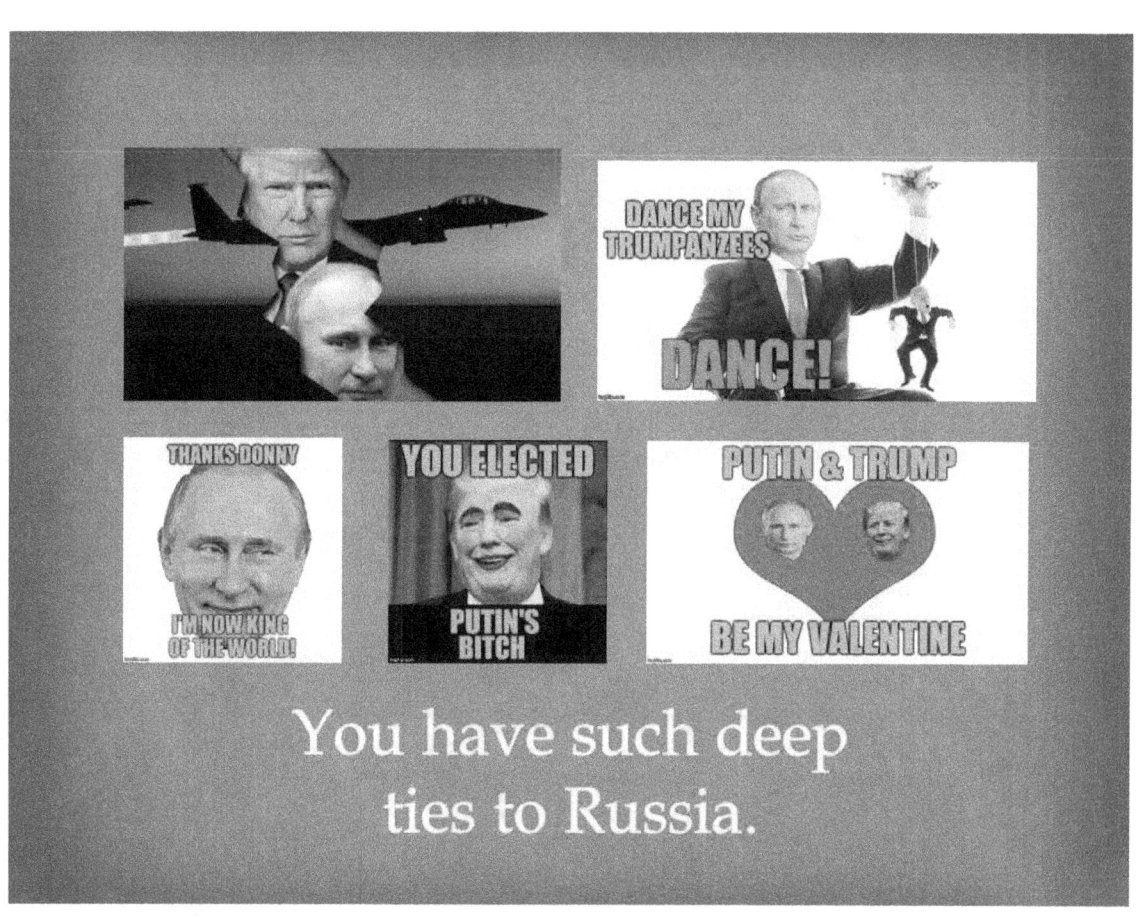

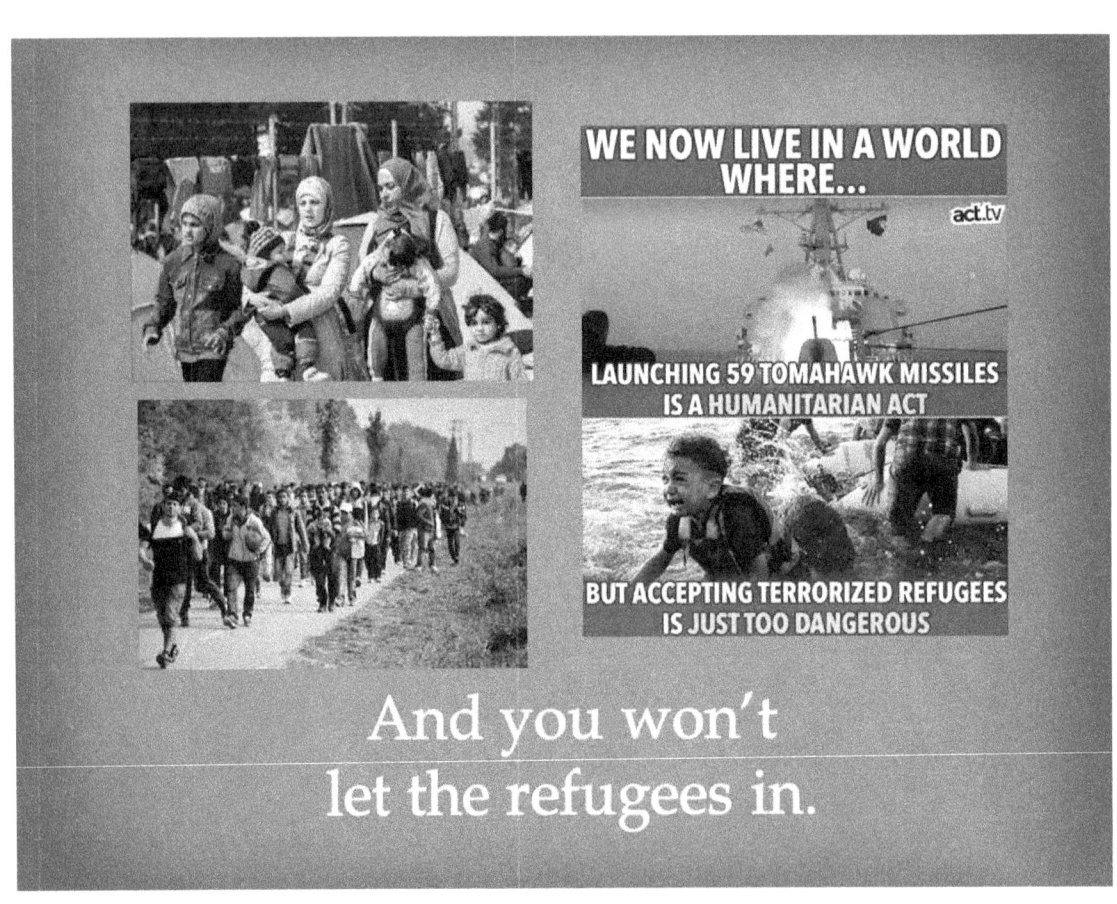

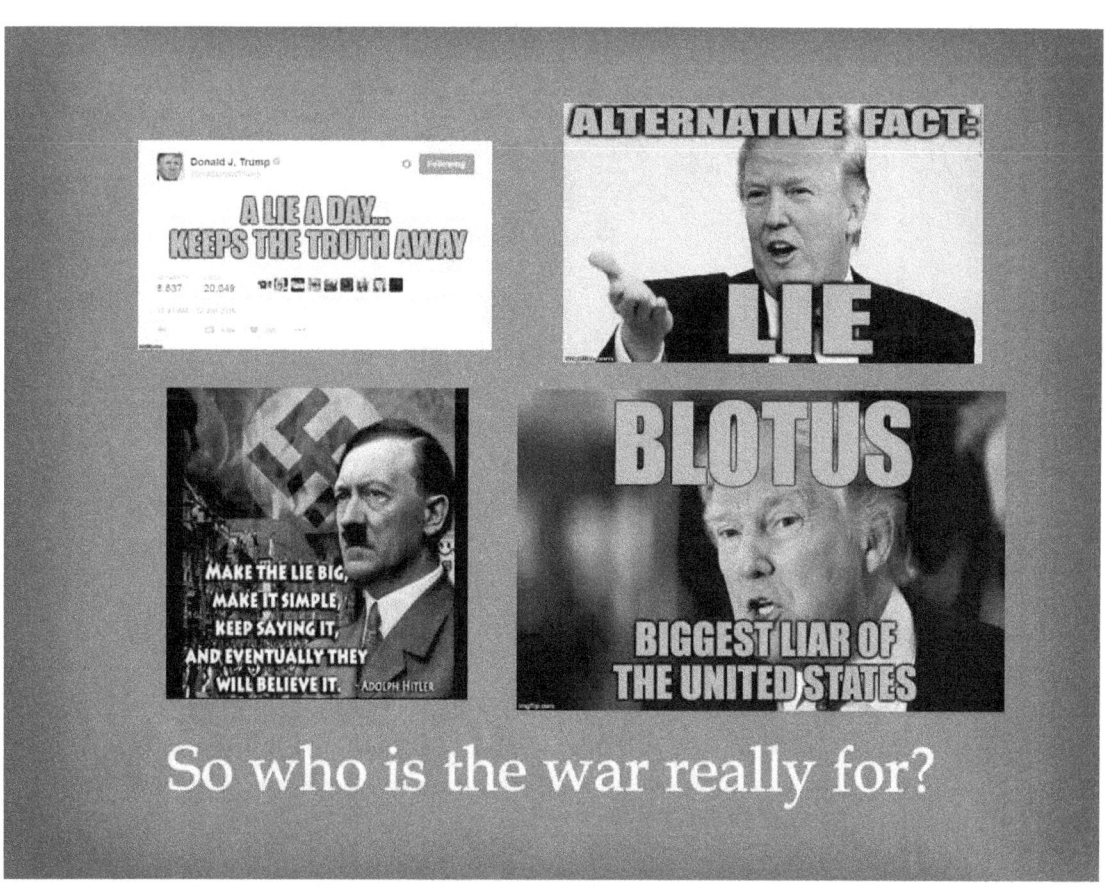

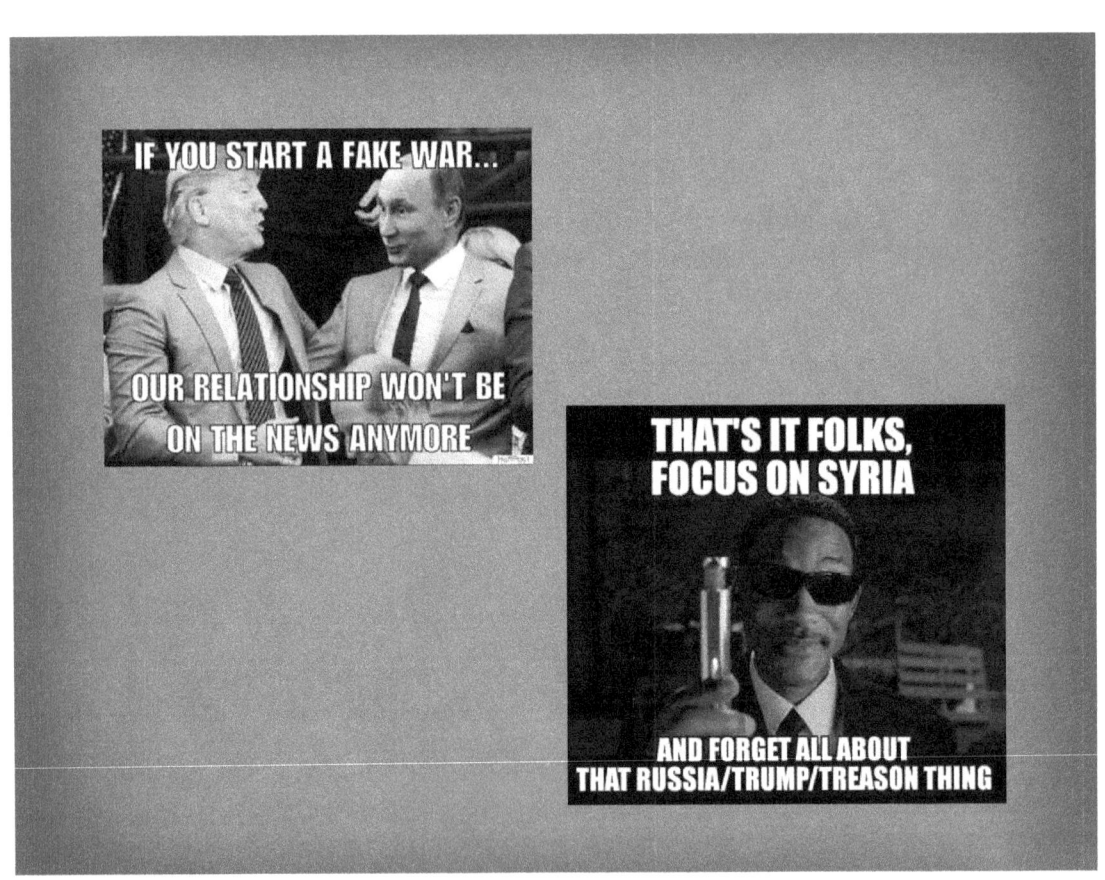

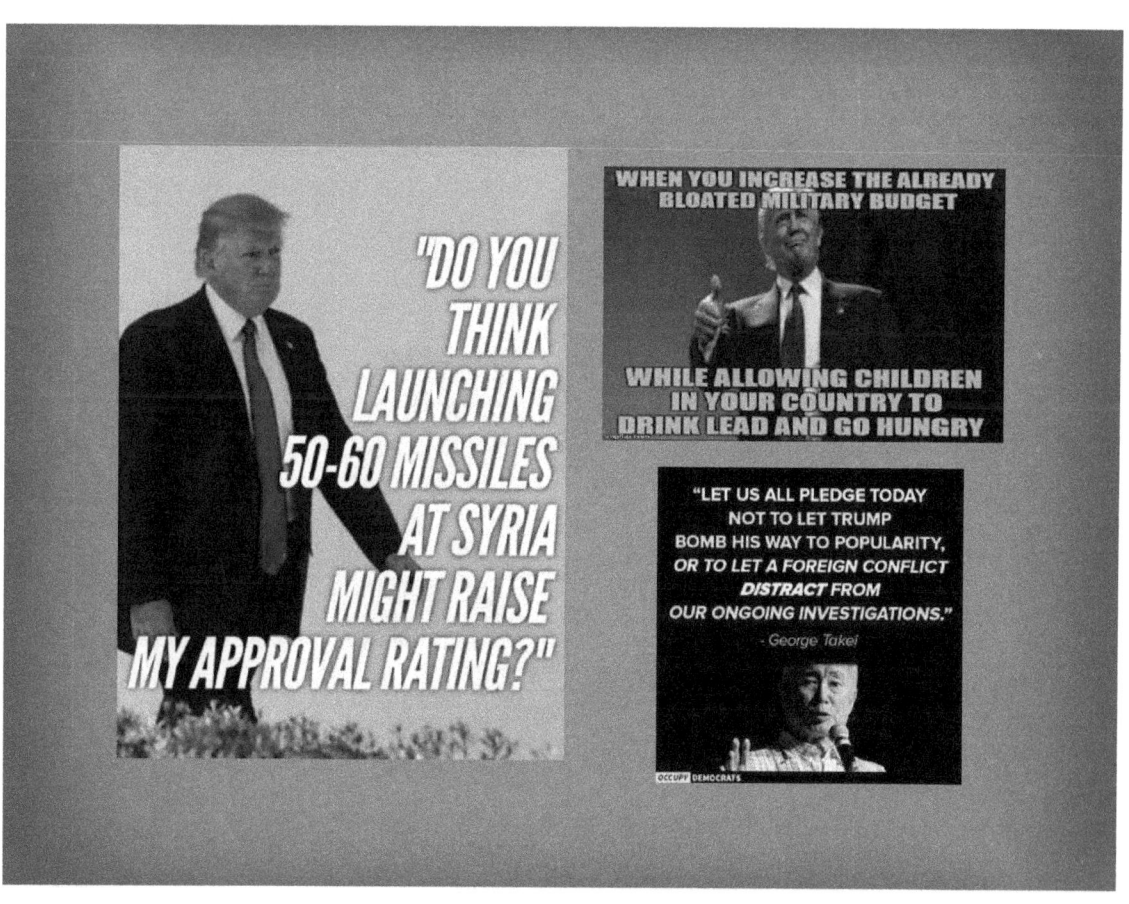

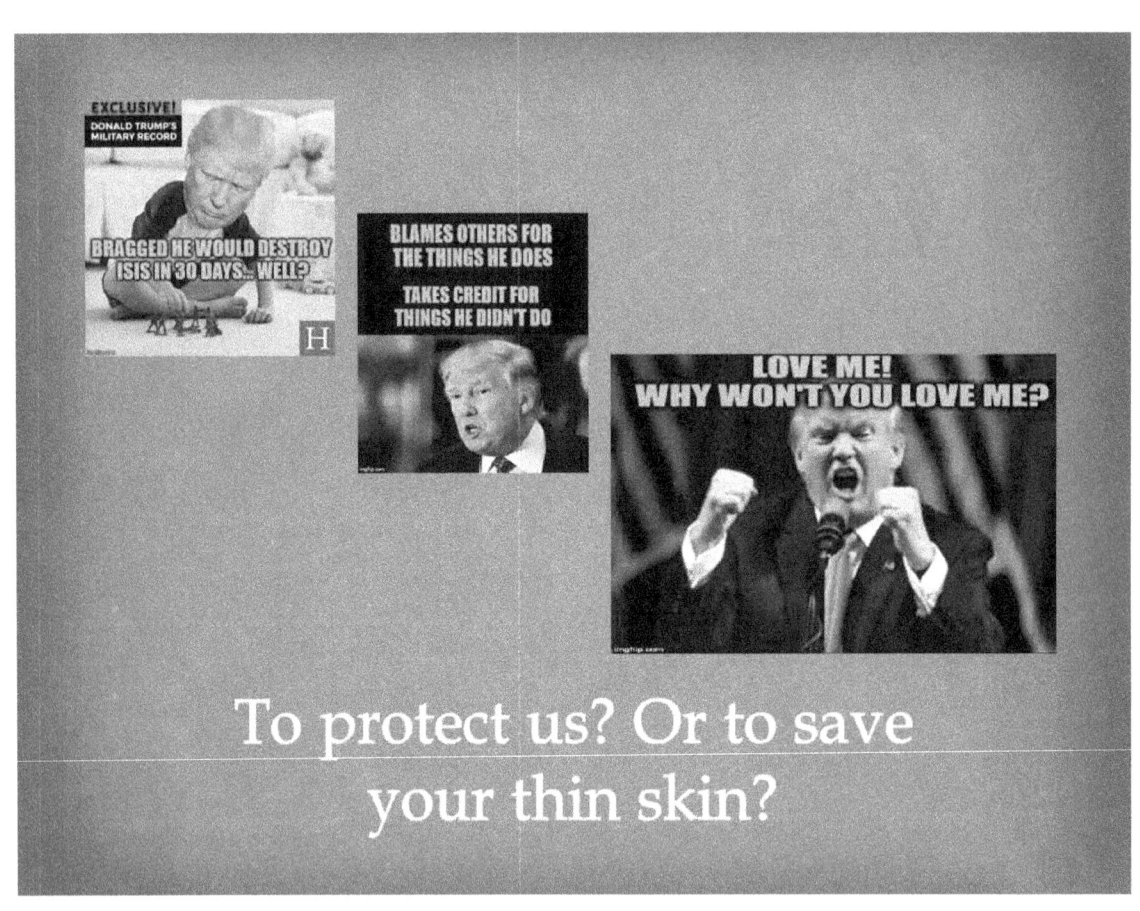

Then, there's the matter of money.

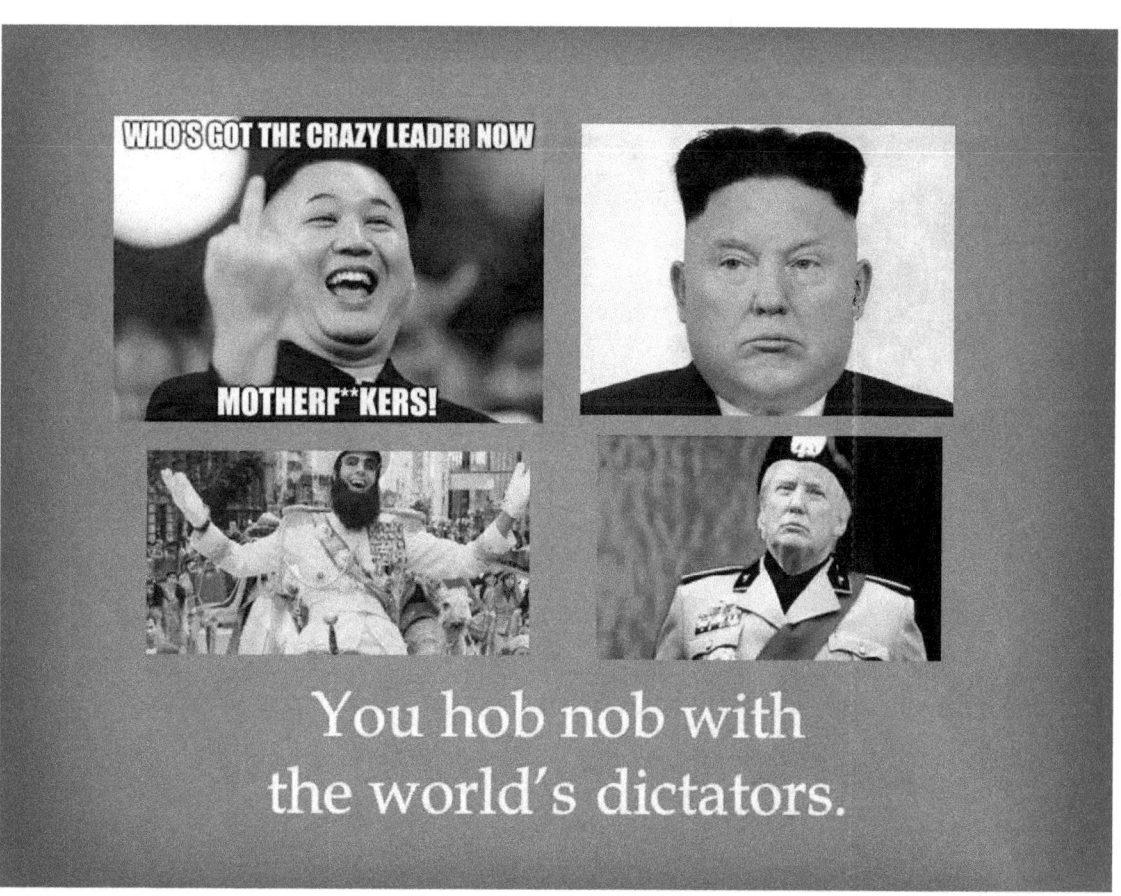

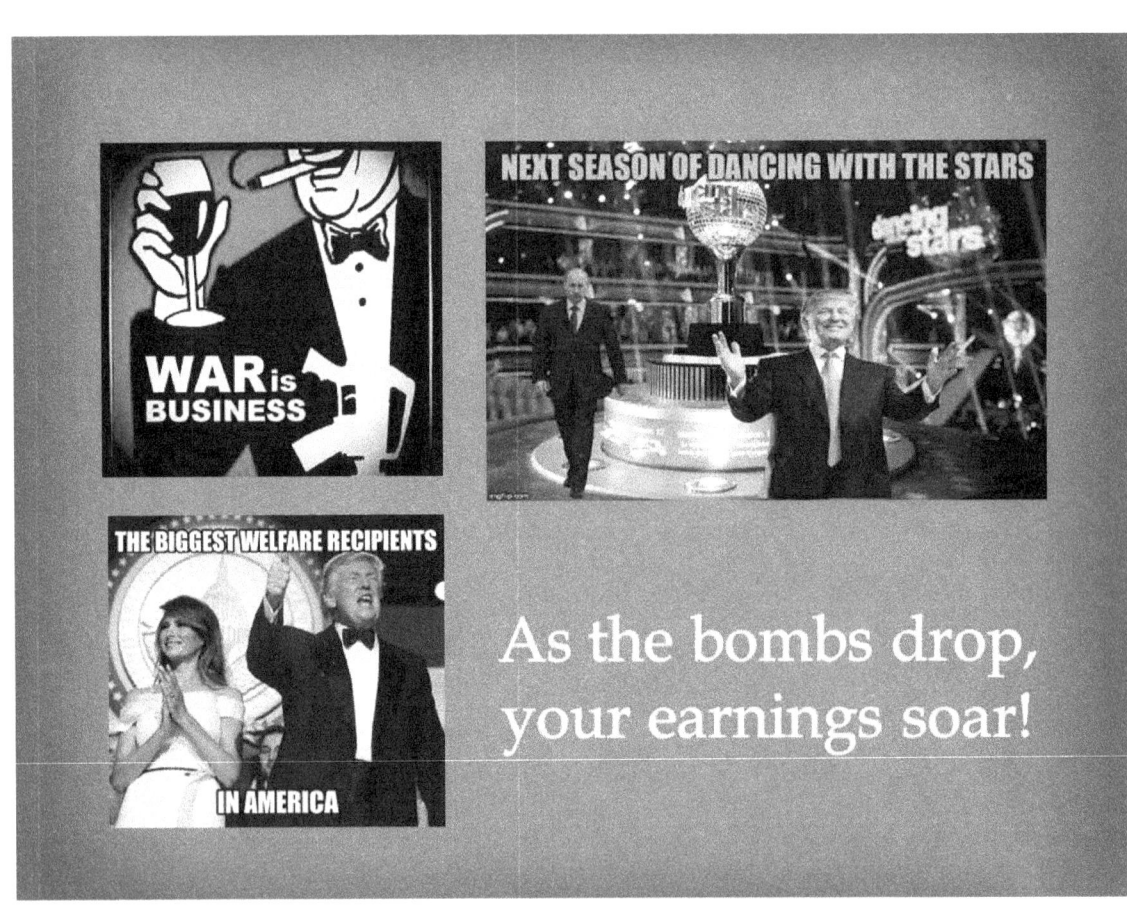

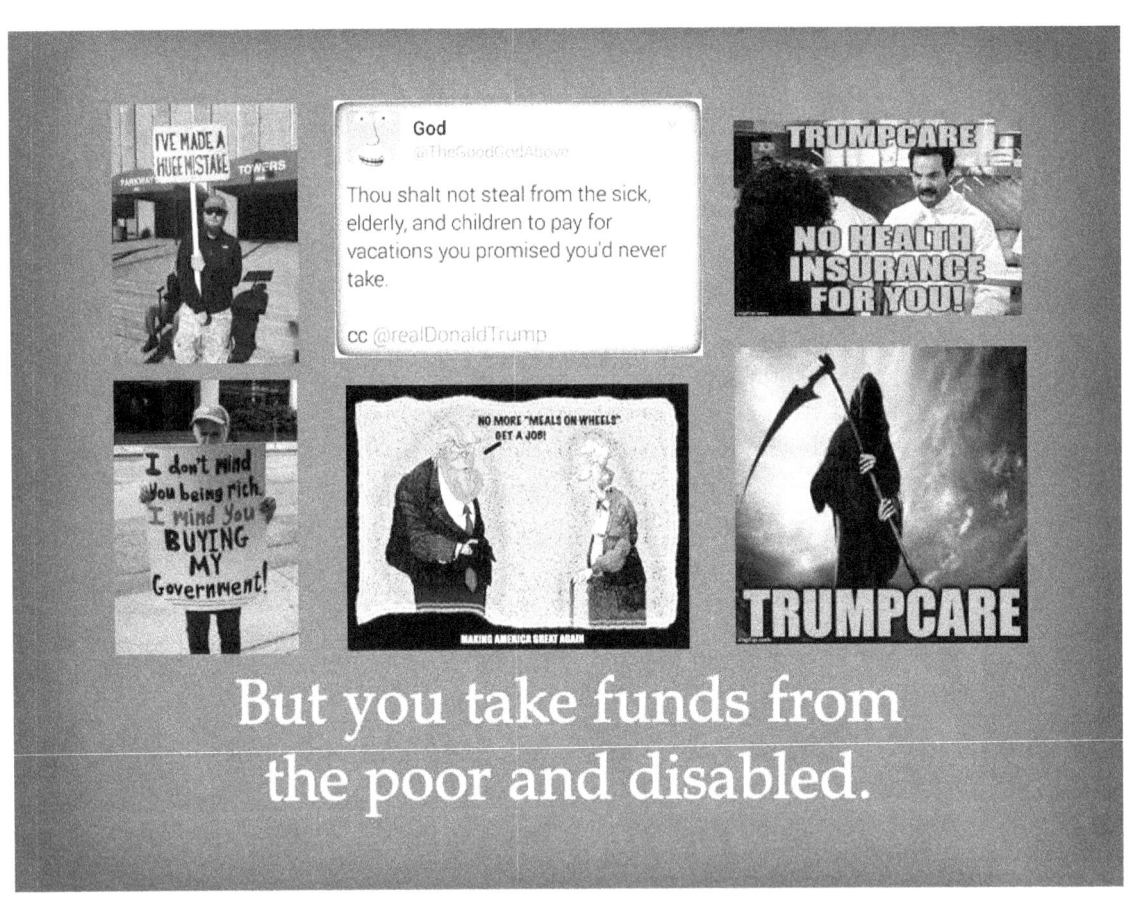

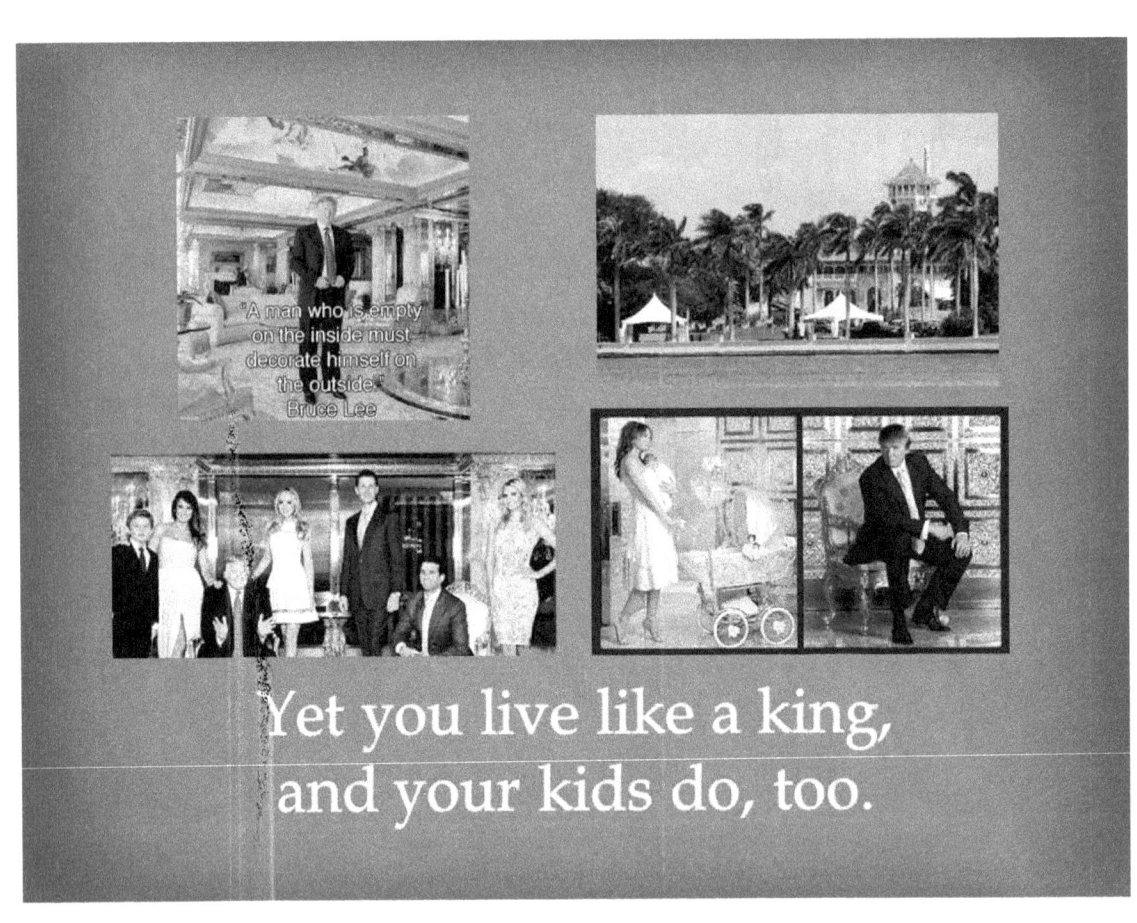

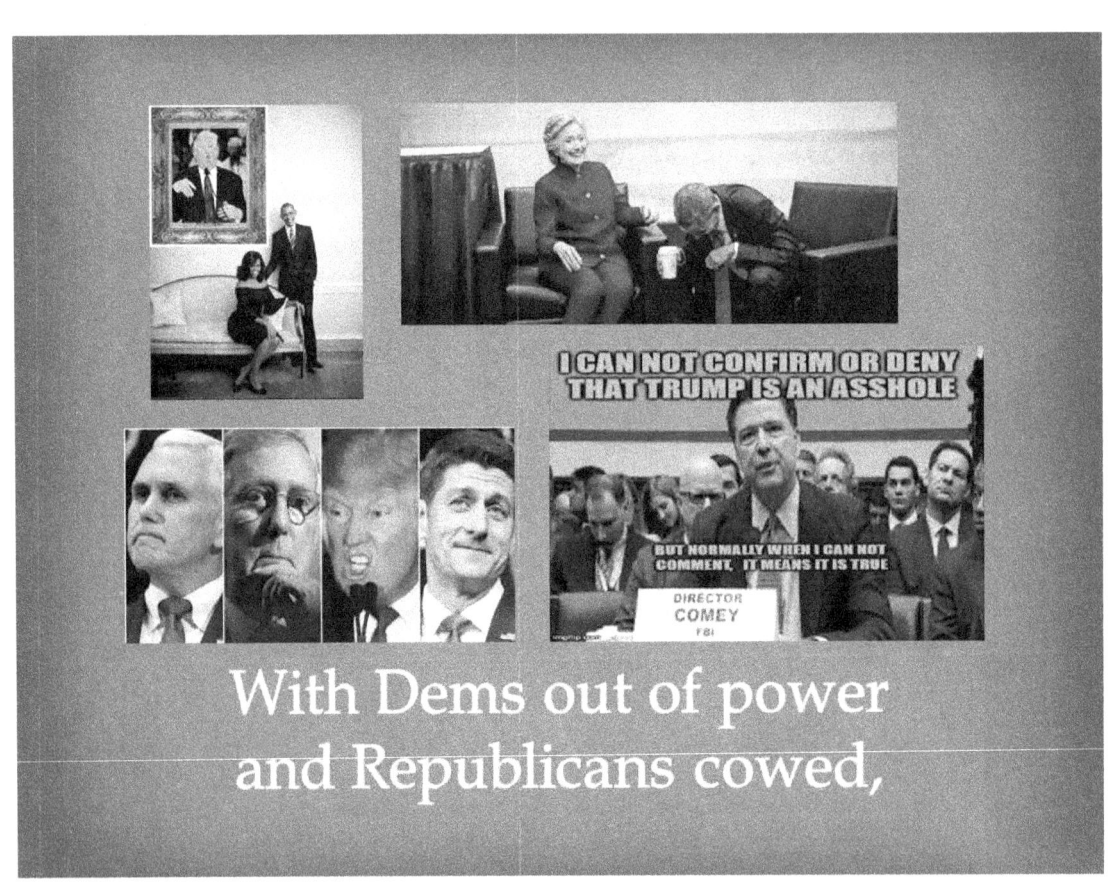

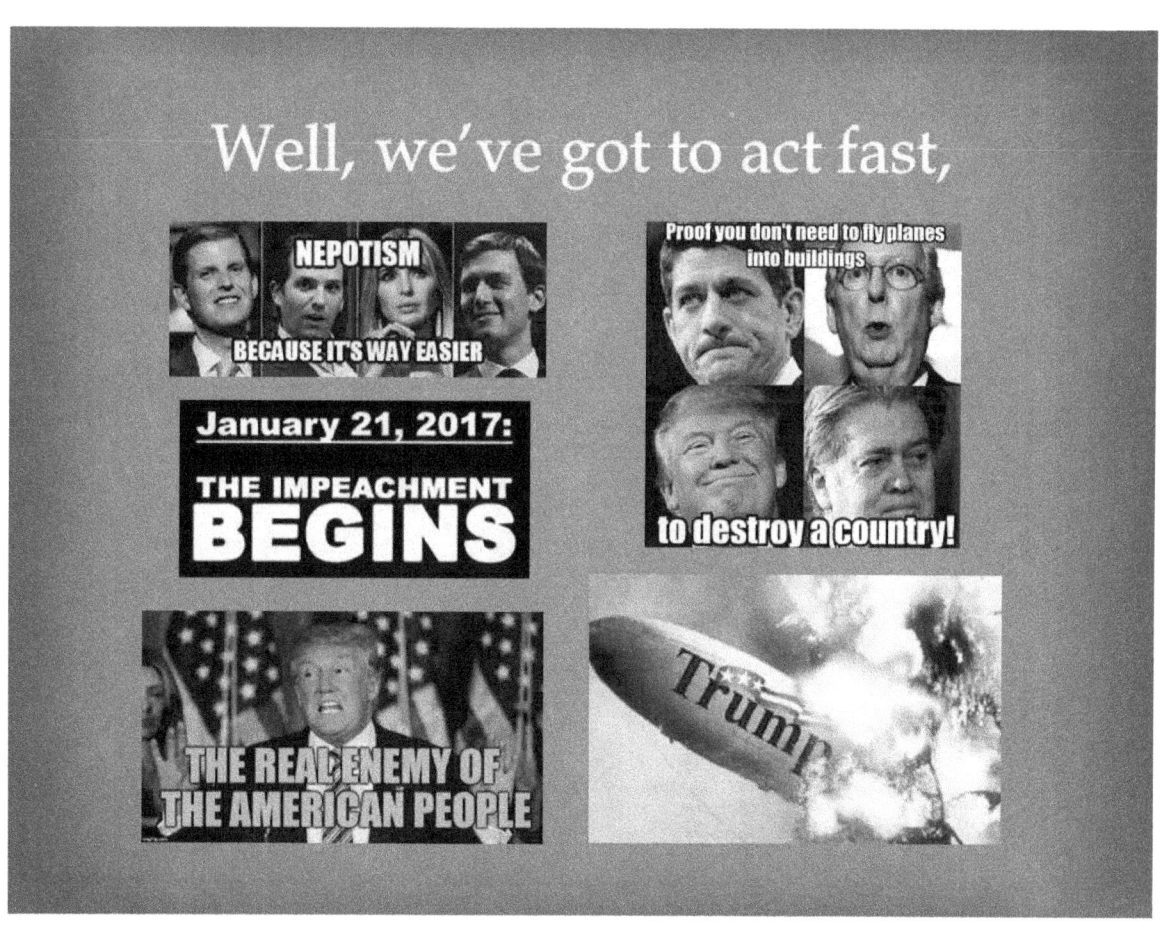

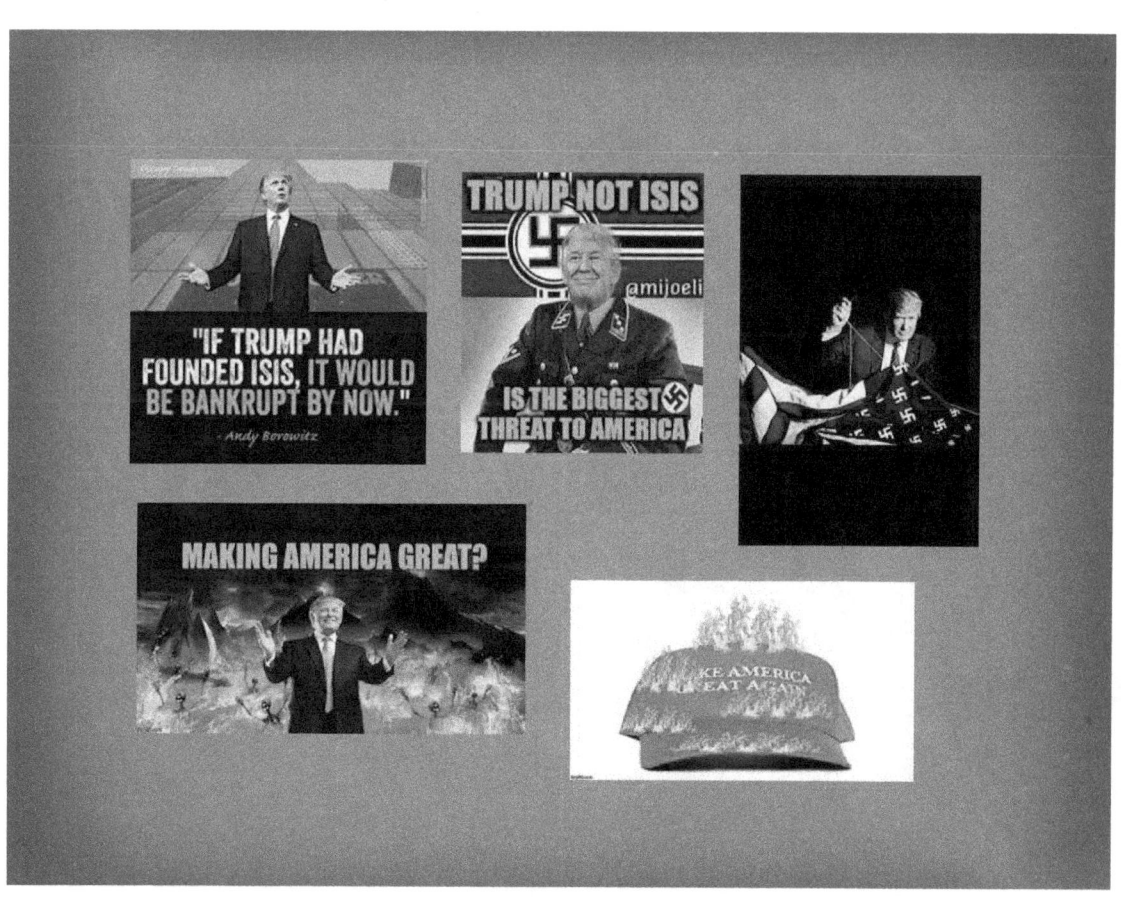

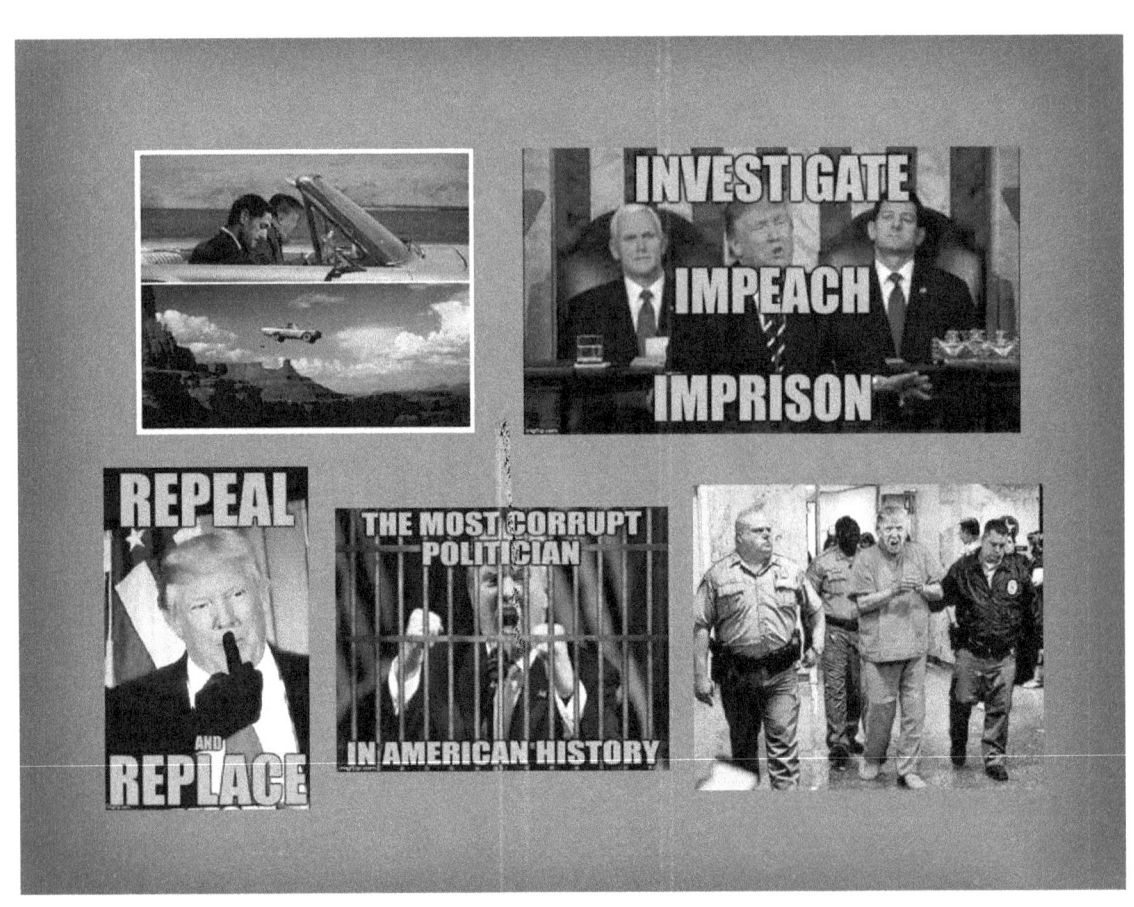

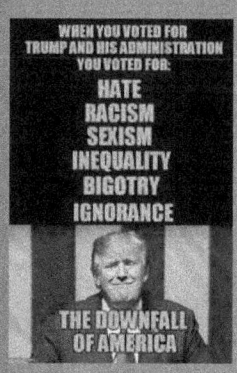

Inspired by:
The idiots and assholes now running or ruining the government...
or running from it.

And thanks to the many photographers and graphic designers whose photos and illustrations inspired the resistance.

PART V: COMMENTARY

TRUMPTY DUMPTY

A Chronicle of Commentary on Trump and the Election

INTRODUCTION

TRUMPTY DUMPTY features a series of columns I wrote on Huffington Post about the dangers of a Trump Presidency not only to the U.S. but to the world.

To begin the series, I wondered why Trump was not attacking the cartoonists and writers who were writing critical articles about him, although he has attacked the media as a whole as the lowest form of humanity and journalists as horrible, disgusting, and dishonest human beings. He has even banned major media publications and networks from getting credentials to cover his events. But he has not gone after a particular individual or filed any lawsuits. Why not?

Then, I began asking if Trump was nuts or mentally deranged, comparing him to animals fighting for power and territory and to nuts (literally), citing the cartoon books I had written: *Trump Is Nuts!*, *Trump Is an Animal!*, and *Who Is Trump, Really?*, with satiric cartoons by illustrator Nick Alexander.

The last column in the series reflects my reaction to the naked Trump statues that appeared in 5 U.S. cities – New York, Los Angeles, San Francisco, Seattle, and Cleveland. Not only was Trump depicted as an overweight, out of shape, paunchy, flabby man to be laughed at and humiliated, much like he made fun of and insulted others, but this status also seemed to be a metaphor for revealing who Trump really was, if only others could see this. He was in effect presented as the "Emperor with No Clothes," which is the same fairy tale that led me to begin commenting on Trump back in February 2016. These comments eventually led to my first book in the series of Trump books: *2016 Election Fairy Tales,* when Trump was still fighting off 16 other candidates in the Republican primaries. Yet many of these tales are still relevant, such as *Little Red Riding Hood and the Big Bad Wolf*, as Hillary battles against the Big Bad Trump.

Thus, since I started with a commentary on a naked Trump with no clothes, it seems only fitting to end this series with my comments in response to the naked Trump statues.

Now, if only these comments can contribute to the election results and preserving American democracy from Trump and his radical right and angry white men minions.

CHAPTER 1: WHY ISN'T TRUMP ATTACKING THE CARTOONISTS AND WRITERS WHO ARE ATTACKING HIM?

During the campaign, Donald Trump has insulted almost everyone he perceives to be against him, including a judge in the Trump University lawsuit for being a Mexican, Mexicans in general, Muslims, a disabled reporter, women, sleazy journalists, you name it.

But the two groups he doesn't seem to have attacked yet are cartoonists drawing insulting cartoons about him – or the people coming up with insulting names for him or passing them on. If you've been following the News Feeds on Facebook, Twitter, or other social media platforms, you know what I mean. In fact, if you Google "Trump cartoons," you'll see 15 or more pages with about 30 cartoons per page.

In the Trump insult cartoons, he has been depicted as Hitler, a screaming baby, and a tycoon reading a book of 2000 insults. He has been portrayed as a nude boxer about to decimate a scared Republican on a tiny elephant, and he has been screaming "I am not a loser!" after he lost the Iowa primary.

In another cartoon, he is wearing a cap saying "Make America Grate (It's Teeth)," and another cartoonist depicted him with a very fat face and a saber, gloating since he just chopped the head off Lady Liberty. In another telling image, he is shown with a huuuge open mouth filled with the bricks of the wall he threatens to build. And soon after he refused to debate Bernie Sanders, myriad images showed Donald's head on the body of a chicken. One of the most graphic showed a photo of a chicken splayed out on a kitchen counter with its legs spread out, and in the hole where the stuffing normally goes was Donald Trump's very fat oily face.

Soon after Trump insulted the Pope, one cartoonist showed a raging Trump with his hair flying and his fists in boxing gloves, so he could take down the Pope, who was on his knees praying. Another cartoon showed Trump decked out like the Pied Piper of Hamelin, leading a bevy of cameramen – presumably off a cliff. Still another image showed Trump with clouds of anger coming out of his ears and nose, and another showed him walking by in his birthday suit as a little kid observes "The Emperor Has No…"

Plus other cartoons show him as a series of monsters, including Trumpenstein and King Kong climbing a skyscraper with a very scared woman in his fist. He is also shown as a Western gunslinger shooting at a Mexican in a sombrero and as a contestant in a pageant, where his bloated half-naked body in a red, white, and blue bathing suit is draped with a large ribbon announcing that he has won the "Mr. USA Bigot" award. Also, he is shown as a baby devil who looks a little like a frog with his face and a forked tail, while a GOP Frankenstein and a Fox News witch look on. Trump is also drawn as Moby Don, a whale determined to build the wall, while some small Mexicans hang on some ropes around his body for dear life. His face has graced many a piñata, too. And many cartoons show him celebrating with Ku Klux Klan members in robes.

Recently, I worked with a cartoonist, Nick Alexander, who created a series of funny images of Trump as one of 27 now extinct beasts and early humans, including the Trumposaurus, Saber Tooth Trump, Neandertrump, and Homo Trumpien, called *Trump Is Extinct…Or May Be Soon!* You can see the full book: *The 2016 Election Follies* on Amazon.

I could go on and on about these Trump cartoons, but you get the idea.

Additionally, there are the many images and names he has been given on the Internet that describe what many voters think of him. Among my favorites are Trumplestilskin, Trumpty Dumpty, Deranged Don, Don the Demented, Don the Dick, Dingleberry Don, and Trump You!

So my question is this. Trump has been attacking everyone who is against him with insults or lawsuits. Even the Republicans who have endorsed him have been getting nervous about his confrontational unprofessional behavior and tirades. Some have refused to endorse him, taken back their endorsements, and even left the party. So, of course, Trump has sought to insult and humiliate them, too.

But why not attack the cartoonists and name callers, who have been attacking him with their pictures and words or both as a racist, bigot, arrogant vulgarian, and maybe insane person who, like Hilary says, is unfit to be the nation's Commander in Chief and have his stubby fingers anywhere near the button.

So far though the cartoonists and writers satirizing Trump have been left unscathed.

However, should Trump get into office, he has threatened to strengthen the libel laws, so perhaps he is waiting until then to go after the cartoonists or writers. Or maybe he might think the cartoonists and writers calling him names are not worth going after, because he thinks their influence is irrelevant or miniscule.

Or is it? Just think of the power of the pen? And remember that a picture says a thousand words.

CHAPTER 2: WHY TRUMP IS LIKE A FIGHTING ANIMAL

Recently there has been talk of how Trump has said he wanted to hit speakers at the Democratic convention who disparaged him "so hard, their heads would spin." Then, he not only suggested that Russia should hack Clinton's emails, which some officials have claimed is akin to treason, but he may have leaked classified information about U.S. having bases in Saudi Arabia which he learned in a news briefing in claiming we shouldn't be paying rent on them.

In short, many of Trump's remarks, especially those about hitting back, are like fighting words to attack, attack, attack to gain power – much like male animals frequently fight other male animals to gain power, territory, and females. For example, Trump is much like a boxing kangaroo, trying to show who's boss, by kicking and jabbing however he can until he defeats a rival. Or he is like a chimp who fights with all the tools he's got, from tree branches to clubs he finds on the ground. When Trump gets on Twitter to spew his hate at different targets, the process is much the same.

In fact, this comparison of Trump to different types of fighting animals is the subject of a recent book: *Trump Is an Animal!: An Illustrated Guide and Coloring Book to the Way that Trump Fights Like Different Types of Animals.* The book combines satirical cartoons with timely critical copy that shows how Trump fights like 21 different animals. Besides kangaroos and chimps, the animals include cunning coyotes, baaad ass baboons, huuuge hippos, charging elephants, mighty meerkats, fighting cocks, penguins, tortoises, and snakes.

The book is the perfect example of how Trump is constantly fighting, often unfairly, with virtually anyone who dares stand up to him. An example is a cartoon and accompanying illustration of Trump as a Huuuge Hippo. In the cartoon, Trump with his very big open mouth confronts a hippo with its huge gaping jaws. The introductory paragraph about Trump reads:

"Hippos are huuuge. Though they are mostly heribvores, they are anything but peaceful vegetarians, since they are highly aggressive and unpredictable and are considered among the most dangerous animals in Africa. As such, they are much like Trump, who responds largely from his intuition and whim, and is ever ready to attack anyone for anything deemed insulting or offensive to him. And he likes everything to be "huuuge," "great," or otherwise "extraordinary."

The rest of the copy in the book is written in a similar vein, briefly describing the different types of animals and the way the males go at it – often in a deadly attack that leaves the loser severely or fatally injured, much like Trump's Republican rivals and the Republican Party as a whole.

Trump Is an Animal! is available on Amazon, and it is part of a series called *Who Is Trump Really?* In fact, a website featuring a half-dozen anti-Trump books has been set up at Who Is Trump Really www.whoistrumpreally.com, also accessible by www.trumpisnuts.net. Other books in the series include *Trump Is Nuts!* and *Trump Is Extinct…Or May Be Soon!.*

One of the reason for writing these books is to help to show Trump for who he really is and contribute to the campaign against him. At least they help to show even more reasons why Trump is unsuited and incompetent to be President, and they may help to broaden the appeal to those who would find the cartoons entertaining as well as informative about the real Trump.

CHAPTER 3: IS TRUMP REALLY NUTS?

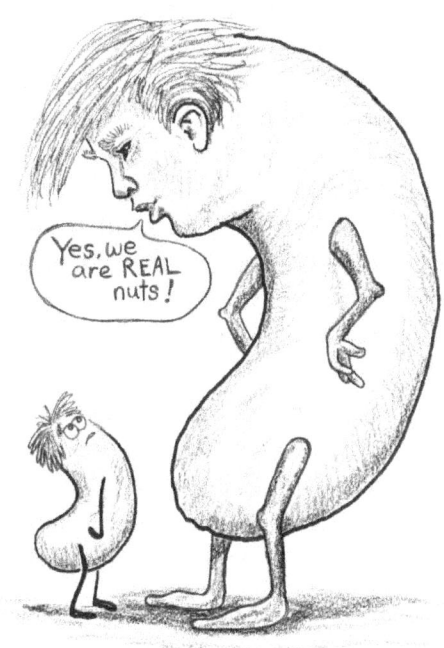

More and more evidence is coming in from the behavior of Donald Trump and the opinions of expert observers that he really is nuts. It seems like Republicans, media commentators, and even psychiatrists have been unwilling to utter the "mentally disturbed" or "mentally ill" designation. They have sought to explain Trump's angry outbursts, erratic behavior, continual lying, confusion about facts, and bullying tactics as due to his narcissistic personality. They have excused his aggressiveness and lack of empathy for others as examples of his hard-nosed business deal tactics. Some have even suggested he has engaged in self-sabotaging tactics because he really doesn't want to win and have to govern.

But more and more, it seems hard to deny. As Daniel Dale of the *Toronto Star* wrote in an article "Is Donald Trump OK? Erratic behavior raises mental health questions," Trump is really not of "sound mind," citing a previous comment by conservative Stephen Hayes in the *Weekly Standard*. Dale also suggested that Michael Bloomberg was alluding to Trump's mental illness when he made this comment in supporting Hillary Clinton: "Let's elect a sane, competent person."

This crazy behavior by Trump is on the world stage for all to see. For example, in an interview with George Stephanopoulos, he rambled on about how Russia wasn't going to go into the Ukraine, when it had two years before, leading to combat between Ukraine and Russia. When asked about the U.S. response to ISIS, he wandered off the subject and talked whether people in the room were good looking. He ranted about how he was no longer friends with Bloomberg and wanted to hit some of the speakers at the Democratic convention very hard. And most famously, he insulted Khizr Khan and his wife by comparing his "sacrifices" in building buildings with their loss of their son

I could go on and on with more examples, but these are not the behaviors of someone who is rational. These are more like the actions and statements of someone with early-stage dementia or Alzheimer's, which are characterized by someone becoming forgetful and increasingly irritable and angry, as they feel themselves losing control. Experts and the general public have generally concluded that he is a narcissist and sociopath, since he has exhibited all the signs associated with these mental and social disorders. Among them are being full of himself, blaming others, not accepting responsibility, thinking he is great and the center of everything, demanding attention, not caring about others, and so on.

But now Trump's behavior goes beyond those traits, as much as Republicans Party members and his loyal Trumpateer followers have been unwilling to see what is increasingly in plain site – like a lurking Pokemon monster. You just need to turn on the program and look in the right direction to see the monster coming closer and closer.

Now, even many Republicans, as well as Democrats, are coming to accept this diagnosis. For instance, Senator Daylin Leach observed: "I think Hillary has to position herself frankly as someone who is sane because that's a contrast…We have a candidate on the other side who literally is, I think, mentally ill." And in TruthDig, Bill Blum observed in "The Psychopathology of Donald Trump" that the issue of Trump's sanity has to be faced. As he pointed out, "Does Donald Trump only *say* crazy things, or does he say crazy things because he actually *is* crazy?" Blum then goes on to point out that the "issue of Trump's emotional stability has also been raised by a growing number of influential and highly respected mental-health practitioners." Even though the American Psychiatric Association advises psychiatrists not to make public statements about public figures who they have not formally evaluated, some psychiatrists have made statements about Trump having a mental disorder out of a sense of urgency. They have done so since the danger is that Trump is only "one election away from being commander in chief of the most powerful nation" on the planet.

No wonder Harry Reid and others have expressed concerns about giving Trump classified information in military briefings and some military leaders have said they will not follow illegal orders to do things, such as torture suspected terrorists or kill their families. Even Mark Cuban, once a supporter, changed his endorsement to Hillary and has called Trump "batshit crazy."

I have observed this growing mental disorder myself, after writing a book about sociopaths: *Lies and Liars: How and Why Sociopaths Lie and How to Detect and Deal with Them.* Then, as the evidence of Trump's crazy behavior mounted, I teamed up with a cartoonist and we wrote *Trump Is Nuts! An Illustrated Guide and Coloring Book on the Many Ways that Trump Has Gone Nuts,* which is also included in the compilation: *Who Is Trump, Really?*, which includes cartoon books comparing Trump to fighting animals and extinct beasts. *The Trump Is Nuts!* book features satiric cartoons depicting Trump as all kinds of nuts from cashews to pecans and ending up as a nut case and in the nuthouse, and it combines these cartoons with incisive commentary about the many ways that Trump's behavior is mentally disturbed or nuts.

For example, in one cartoon, Trump is drawn as a peanut in a nut case with Hitler and Mussolini, and includes this commentary:

"Is Trump really a nut case? That's what more and more people believe, including some psychologists who have described him as having a 'narcissistic personality disorder," whereby one thinks that everything is about me, me, me. Someone with this disorder also has delusions of grandeur about who one is and what one can do…He always has to win, whatever he does and makes excuses should he lose at anything, so he still comes out on top."

I wrote that in a book that was published on June 23rd, and now Trump's symptoms seem even worse. So is Trump nuts? I think the signs are all there that he truly is. So now the question becomes what are we as the American people going to do about it? If we truly let him anywhere near the Oval Office, we are truly nuts, too!

CHAPTER 4: DOES TRUMP HAVE EARLY-STAGE ALZHEIMER'S?

Increasingly, in response to Donald Trump's recent behavior, many people are asking if he is really mentally deranged, and some commentators have wondered if he might have early- stage Alzheimer's. These questions haven't yet made it to the mainstream media. They have mainly been confined to web publications and commentators on Facebook and other social media sites. But now psychologists and psychiatrists are being asked these questions, at a time when many Republicans and other political leaders are disavowing Trump, and the Republican Party is exploring what to do if Trump pulls out of the race. Trump has even been hinting that he may bail by suggesting that Pence will handle foreign and domestic affairs; that the election is rigged; that he would withdraw if the polls drop; and that there could be civil disobedience if he loses.

The evidence of craziness has been coming fast and furious for the past few days, especially since Trump began attacking Khizr Khan and his wife, who are considered Gold Star parents, since they lost their son in Iraq in 2004, well before Obama came into office or Clinton became Secretary of State. But no matter. Trump has suggested that Obama was responsible for the son's death, that Khan is an agent for the Muslim Brotherhood. Trump has even continued to up his attacks at a time when many members of the Republican Party have disavowed his comments and announced that they can no longer vote for him, due to his increasingly out of control behavior and because they feel one should not attack Gold Star parents, who have sacrificed so much in losing their son.

Plus there have been many other crazy incidents. One recent incident occurred in a security briefing when he asked three times why the USA can't use nuclear weapons, if we have them. In an interview with ABC's George Stephanopoulos, he asserted that Russia wouldn't go into the Ukraine, and when Stephanopoulos explained that Russia had already gone there, he tried to explain his way out of the situation. Then, when a baby cried at a recent rally, Trump first talked about loving babies and about a minute later, he kicked the mother and baby out of the rally.

Anyone following the news will see the pattern – increasingly erratic behavior, and despite calls to act more presidential, exercise control, show empathy, and focus his attacks on Hillary, Trump seems more and more to simply react emotionally by attacking anyone who has said anything negative about him. He even has withdrawn his support from Paul Ryan and John McCain, since they criticized his attack on the Khans, and he withdrew press credentials from the *New York Times*, because they don't write "good."

I previously cited authors who raised questions about Trump's mental health and suggested he is mentally ill and called him crazy. Now, pointing to his erratic behavior, a growing chorus suggests that one reason for this crazy behavior is that Trump has early-stage Alzheimer's. According to the Alzheimer's Association, the 10 early signs and symptoms of Alzheimer's include these: a memory loss that disrupts daily life; challenges in planning or solving problems, which includes difficulty in concentrating, and difficulty in completing familiar tasks at work or leisure. Other signs are having decreased or poor judgment and changes in mood or personality.

One can certainly see examples of this in Trump's recent behavior. For example, he forgot about Russia taking over the Ukraine and he has difficulty staying on the subject in his interviews and rallies, skipping from one topic to another. He has repeatedly asked for the same information over and over, such as asking about using nuclear weapons three times, and has problems in finding the right word or calling things by the wrong names in his tweets. He has shown very poor judgment in his recent attacks, and he has been increasingly on edge and ready to attack. Much like a classic patient with early-stage Alzheimer's, he readily becomes suspicious, fearful, or anxious, so he fights back like an animal or child, governed by the limbic system, the source of emotions, rather than exercising control, which is a function of the higher brain faculties. There is also research that Alzheimer's is hereditary, and his father, Fred Trump, who lived from 1905 to 1999, suffered from Alzheimer's for six years before he became sick with pneumonia in June 1999 and died a few weeks later.

So given Trumps behavior, questions have been raised as early as July 2015, though not yet widely discussed in the mainstream media. For example, in the Daily Mail online forum, one established poster, Neil Cavuto, a TV announcer and commentator on the Fox Business Network made this observation: "Donald Trump claims to have a good memory, perhaps he did before the Alzheimer's, because it isn't open to interpretation…Early signs of Alzheimer's would explain quite a bit of Donald Trump's recent behavior. He has proven thin skinned. He has behaved erratically and shown little regard for social conventions – for example his attack on Megyn Kelly claiming she was asking difficult questions because she was menstruating and his mocking of a reporter's disability."

Another poster on this board Jack N Gary had this to say: "Does Trump show he's having trouble with speech and turning thoughts into words or understanding others. Well, we've seen his off topic rants when asked a question…When asked a simple question on taxes by Sean Hannity – a known Trump supporter – he went on a verbal meander that brought in Russia, China, ISIS and hedge fund managers without actually addressing the question."

Then, in February 2016, a series of commentators addressed the question: "Is Donald Trump Suffering from Delusional Senile Dementia?" The article by News Corpse noted that the "very public meltdown of Donald Trump over the past few months" raised the question of whether he was a likely candidate for a diagnosis of dementia. To support this viewpoint, the article gave examples of Trump's impaired judgment, loss of memory, and childish behavior. For example, even before the Khan eruption, at the beginning of his campaign he made some outrageous statements "untethered to reality" such as suggesting Mexico was sending over rapists and murders and that John McCain was not a war hero because he got captured. Though Trump bragged about having one of the best memories, he claimed he had seen thousands and thousands of Muslims celebrating the collapse of the World Trade Center which never happened, forgot that he once praised both Clinton and Obama highly, and claimed he never met a disabled reporter he mocked, though they had met many times. Then, of course, there are Trump's numerous childish tantrums, marked by "infantile insults about people's looks and character," and if criticized he punches back with "baseless, often unrelated, rebuttals."

Later, in April 2016, writing for the Inquisitor, Samantha Kilgore asked the question: "Does Donald Trump Have Alzheimer's? Questions About GOP Frontrunner's Mental Fitness Arise." As Kilgore notes, according to the Alzheimer's Association, if two or more 'core mental functions' seem impaired, that individual "should seek medical help in order to get screened for possible dementia." And Trump has been having trouble with at least five core functions: memory, communication and language, ability to focus and pay attention, and reasoning and judgment. Plus she notes that that "people suffering Alzheimer's have difficulty remembering newly learned information, are often disoriented, have mood and behavior changes, an increasing sense of paranoia and suspicion, and a deepening confusion about events, time, and places. In particular, she points out how Trump's language is often disjointed, such as when he said in the first debate: "We need brain in this country to turn it around." In another case, at a rally in Pittsburgh, Trump asked about a Penn State football coach Joe Paterno, who was disgraced due to his involvement in a sexual abuse scandal, died in 2012, and has no connection to Pittsburgh. Even so, Trump asked "How's Joe Paterno? We gonna bring that back." Another time, in New York, he mixed up the September 11 tragedy with the 7/11 convenience store.

Finally, for one more example, in April 27, 2016, April Hamlin writing for the If You Only News website raised this question: "Maybe Trump Isn't Just an *sshole, Could He Actually Be Suffering from Alzheimer's or Dementia." Among other things she cited Trump's response to a *Washington Post* reporter who asked if he would consider using a tactical nuclear weapon against ISIS. Trump awkwardly replied, shifting the subject in no particular logical way: "I don't want to use, I don't want to start the process of nuclear. Remember the one thing that everybody has said, I'm a counterpuncher. Rubio hit me. Bush hit me. When I said low energy, he's a low-energy individual, he hit me first. I spent, by the way, he spent 18 million dollars' worth of negative ads on me." When the Post reporter tried to get him back on topic, Trump replied: "I'll tell you one thing, this is a very good-looking group of people here. Could I just go around so I know who the hell I'm talking to?"

And now it would seem Trump is becoming even nuttier, which is to be expected as the symptoms of mental deterioration in Alzheimer's become increasingly worse. As Daniel Halper noted in an August 3, 2016 article in the *New York Post*, members of Trump's presidential campaign say he has been getting "nuttier and nuttier," so that they are "increasingly frustrated by his outrageous comments and behavior."

In short, since at least July 2015, the evidence has been mounting and questions have been raised about Trump's mental health. And now? Well, follow the news for yourself, and see what you think. I think his behavior and statements show the classic signs of early-stage Alzheimer's which will only get worse. So should Trump be in the Oval Office? Should he have the ability to push the nuclear button? We could be one insult away from any foreign leader saying something to rile Trump, and then boom! It could be the beginning – or the end – of World War III.

Want more examples of how Trump is going nuts? To illustrate, I teamed up with a cartoonist and we wrote *Trump Is Nuts! An Illustrated Guide and Coloring Book on the Many Ways that Trump Has Gone Nuts* and *Trump Is An Animal! Trump Is Nuts!* features satiric cartoons depicting Trump as all kinds of nuts from cashews to pecans and ending up as a nut case and in the nuthouse. It combines these cartoons with incisive commentary about the many ways that Trump's behavior is mentally disturbed or nuts. *Trump Is an Animal!* features Trump as a number of animals, from kangaroos to chimps and fur seals, who are fighting for power, territory, and mates, much like Trump strikes out and fights with anyone who threatens his position.

CHAPTER 5: PRO-TRUMPERS RESPOND TO THE QUESTION: "DOES TRUMP HAVE EARLY- STAGE ALZHEIMER'S?"

Now that my post: "Does Trump Have Early-Stage Alzheimer's?" has reached over 1.3 thousand likes, I found it intriguing to see the wide range of responses. They essentially fell into two camps. One was those who found the article reinforced their anti-Trump attitude and view that Trump really was nuts. The other camp was the Trump supporters who responded by attacking the "liberal" media, trashed the Huff Post, and accused Hillary for lying and being equally or more crazy. A few claimed I was "just a writer and no expert," although my article primarily cited authorities on the topic.

I even got a message from one Trump supporter who stated that he was with a film production company and received an email from my company about a film project. He went on to say "So you know Donald J. Trump is my cousin" and complained that my Changemakers Publishing site was trashing him. He thought I "should no (sic) – nothing personal just business." Was that an implied threat about not doing business together – or something more? I promptly took his company out of my database to be sure he didn't get any emails from me or my associate.

I got the responses to my post in two ways. One way was by posting links to my Huffington Post article on Facebook posts of negative news stories and articles about Trump. The other way was promoting my post on my Changemakers Publishing page through a small Facebook ad campaign, where I found that many respondents were fervent pro-Trumpers and ready to bash anyone who dared to question his abilities or sanity. While some responses were directly in response to my article, others were part of a continuing conversation in which I posted a link to my article. In any case, I found it interesting to see the big split in the responses. I have not included any names to protect the identity of the commentators, though you might find them in the Facebook archives.

So here goes, starting with the Trump defenders, many of whom probably didn't read my article, since they didn't understand what it meant to suggest that Trump might have early-stage Alzheimer's, based on the Alzheimer's Association's description of the 10 core symptoms. These were references by many of the authorities I cited to support my suggestion that Trump showed over half the signs of this illness, including a memory loss that disrupts daily life, difficulty in concentrating, having decreased or poor judgment, and changes in mood or personality. I gave plenty of examples of Trump's recent behavior to support this viewpoint, such as Trump forgetting about Russia taking over the Ukraine, his difficulty in staying on a subject, and his being increasingly on edge, paranoid, and ready to attack, like an animal or child.

One way to dispute an unwanted message is to attack the messenger, which many Trump defenders did by attacking the media. As one Trumpkin commented: "Are there no depths too low for the media? Answer: no, there are not." Another proclaimed: "You morons in the media…You have to stop with all this made up crap & grow up and be journalists not writers for the National Enquirer, but then again at least the(sic) admit they fudge the truth, the mainstream media should be ashamed of themselves…Just saying." Another commented: "God the kooks are desperate to endlessly push this garbage."

Some tried to attack the reputation of the Huffington Post by calling it "tabloid journalism," despite its illustrious roster of experts and authorities. As one Trumpeteer proclaimed: "You guys at huff and puff have it full brown," to which another Trumpeteer added: "What lies!! Sickening…", a sentiment echoed by another supporter who said: "Apparently journalism is dead," and another who proclaimed: "Huff Post is not journalism." Still another Trumpkin blasted the Huffington Post as "a liberal propaganda site spreading lies filtered through the ass of George Soros."

Some seemed to think the media revelations about Trump actually helped him by backfiring on the media, though they were clearly wrong, and rather showed their own ignorance by responding with unsupported and uninformed posts. As one Trump defender put it: "The funny thing is that you people at the H Post actually think this kind of crap hurts him when it actually helps him because the more you spew your bullshit, the more we can see how corrupt the system is and support for Trump grows…what idiots you people are."

Other Trumpkins sought to counterpunch by turning an attack on Trump into an attack on Hillary, the Clintons, and the Democrats, frequently citing inaccurate information and writing in barely literate English. For example, some of their comments were:

"I see a rabid DEM write this inflammatory piece of crapola lol."

"People will NOT forget what the DNC did no matter how much TRUMP does whatever and says whatever. That does NOT negate what she did to sanders. AND more emails are being released."

"Media and Obama and Hillary are just making anything up too (sic) stop trump and the American people."

"Nothing wrong with Trump but Hillary has some pretty serious mental issues, that I am sure."

"Hillary has seizures on a daily basis."

"The actual evidence is…KilLIARy Clinton suffering from epilepsy caused by issues in her brain like tumors, strokes…and evidence by multiple bouts of dizziness, fainting, and lethargy. She also looks like Evi Lyn's even older aunt and has the same mentality of Skeletor."

"The DEVIL wants Hillary."

"Hillary is a thief and a liar."

"Trump is sharp as a tack. Killary is an enormous risk to our national security and our freedoms. Vote Trump, the only one not already bought and paid for by people who hate us. P.S. She has a trail of destruction and dishonesty, but most importantly she has blood on her hands! Such a disgrace. Go Trump! Make American Great Again!!!"

"Trump…is the lesser of two evils. He speaks his mind, he is not part of the establishment, and he does not give in to lobbyists. Oblama and Hitlary are trying their best to turn American into a Socialist country."

Still other respondents were so anti-Hillary that they believed that Trump was a Hillary plant, designed to say such outrageous things that he would lose the election and Hillary would win. In their view, Trump was simply acting as if he was nuts, but wasn't really, so it was all part of an entertainment game for a political end. As one respondent replied to my question about Trump having early-stage Alzheimer's?" "Nonsense. He's working with the Clintons." Still another posted that the whole battle didn't really matter, because "Everyone from opposing political parties deposits their money in the same banks. Guess who's really getting paid."

In short, the Trump supporters were ready to put down the media for bringing a message they didn't want to hear, or they attacked like Trump to denigrate Hillary, with the actual facts of little concern. They were just hurling damaging information against her based on rumor, innuendo, and misinformation, and they turned any questions about Trump's mental health into questions about the mental ability of Hillary and anyone who might dare to question Trump's mental fitness. Some even accused Hillary of treason and seeking to undermine America. By contrast, as I'll describe in a subsequent article, the anti-Trumpers were generally more well-informed and literate in responding and citing other sources they had read.

Given this ongoing election battle, I have written a series of articles and books about Trump and the election out of a genuine concern about the future of the United States and the potential damages Trump could inflict on America and the world, should he become the most powerful person as President of the United States.

You can see more examples of the dangers Trump presents in the books I have written. A listing of the full series is at Who Is Trump Really? www.whoistrumpreally.com (also accessible from www.trumpisnuts.net and www.trumpisanut.com. For my most recent books, I teamed up with a cartoonist and we wrote *Trump Is Nuts! An Illustrated Guide and Coloring Book on the Many Ways that Trump Has Gone Nuts* and *Trump Is An Animal! Trump Is Nuts!* features satiric cartoons depicting Trump as all kinds of nuts from cashews to pecans and ending up as a nut case and in the nuthouse. The book combines cartoons with incisive commentary about the many ways that Trump's behavior is mentally disturbed or nuts. *Trump Is an Animal!* features Trump as a number of animals, from kangaroos to chimps and fur seals, who are fighting for power, territory, and mates, much like Trump strikes out and fights with anyone who threatens his position.

CHAPTER 6: TRUMP IS A NUT WEBSITE ECHOES VIEW OF REPUBLICAN INSIDER

"Trump is a nut, and he likes to surround himself with nuts," said Stuart Stevens, who ran Mitt Romney's 2012 presidential campaign, in an article in the latest August 22-28 *Bloomberg Businessweek*. Stevens was commenting on the choice of Donald Trump's latest campaign manager, Steve Bannon, formerly the executive chairman of *Breitbart News*, which is known for its support of the "nationalist, racially paranoid splinter group of anti-establishment conservatives who have rallied to Trump's banner."

Steven's remark is even reflected in a website of the same name: Trump Is a Nut (www.trumpisanut.com), also accessible through the Trump Is Nuts name. (www.trumpisanut.net). Coincidentally, the website has already been up for nearly two months, and it is the title of a book: *Trump Is a Nut!* published on June 23 with a five star Amazon review. So Stevens' comment reflects what a growing number of people have been thinking – that Trump is not merely a danger to American democracy by creating a dictatorship but actually "nuts". In fact, in the *Bloomberg Businessweek* article, writer Joshua Green notes that the goal of hiring Bannon, profiled in the magazine as "The Most Dangerous Political Operative in America." was to unshackle Trump even more. In this way, Trump could unleash his inner Trump and go full anti-establishment and anti-Washington to fire up his supporters.

No wonder several dozen Republicans, including former RNC officials, have publically turned against Trump's nomination and are urging the party to cut off Trump's funding in order to redirect it to endangered House and Senate candidates. Moreover, Stevens has suggested that the Republican end game is like the "bunker scene in *Downfall*, only the Trump crowd won't tell Hitler the truth. It's utter madness." But then, that's because Stevens thinks "Trump is a nut," just like the *Trump Is a Nut!* cartoon book and the Trump Is a Nut website (www.trumpisanut.com) have been saying for nearly two months

Both the book and website were developed by author/sociologist Gini Graham Scott, Ph.D., who has been closely following the election for the past six months and has written seven books about Trump, now featured on the Trump Is a Nut website. In the tongue-in-cheek cartoon book *Trump Is Nuts!*, Scott compares Trump to a series of nuts from peanuts to pecans and shows him ending up in a nut case with two noted dictators – Hitler and Mussolini, and finally he is hauled off to a nut house. The *Trump Is Nuts!* book is on Amazon and Kindle, while the cartoons are featured in a video on Pivotshare. The book is also part of a trilogy called *Who Is Trump, Really,* which includes the books: *Trump Is Extinct – Or May Be Soon!* and *Trump Is an Animal*, which compare Trump respectively to extinct beasts and early humans and to fighting animals, like the kangaroo and chimpanzee.

So is Trump really nuts? Could Trump just be playing a nutty character, like a person on a reality show? Could his crazy words and behaviors be due to the onset of Alzheimer's, since they seem to match 6 of the 10 core symptoms, according to the Alzheimer's Association? Or are Trump's antics just part of a long-time aggressive, thin-skinned personality? It's a question raised by Dr. Gini Graham Scott in an article "Does Trump Have Early-Stage Alzheimer's," on the Huffington Post, which gotten over 1.3 thousand likes http://tinyurl.com/z64hltk. In the article, she cites numerous experts, authorities, and writers who have suggested that one reason for Trump's crazy behavior is that he has early-stage Alzheimer's. Whatever the answer to these questions, Stevens, along with many others, think that "Trump is a nut," who is surrounded by many other nuts. And that appears to be a reason that his poll numbers are going down, down, down, because increasingly people fear having a nut in the White House or anywhere near a nuclear button.

CHAPTER 7: THE NAKED TRUMP STATUES SHOW TRUMP'S TRUE NATURE

The naked Trump statues erected on August 18 in five cities – New York, Los Angeles, San Francisco, Seattle, and Cleveland – have become a virtual meme for Trump and his candidacy. They not only show off Trump in all his naked glory, but they show through the expression of the artist what millions of people in America and around the world think of Trump. More and more, people see him as a national joke and embarrassment, although what he represents is not so funny – a racist, bigoted, isolationist, paranoid vision of America. These statues represent one more statement that Trump is really just a lumpy overweight potbellied man who presents himself to the world with orange make-up. But underneath, he is stark naked.

Even the New York Parks Department, upon hauling the statue away -- fittingly in the back of a dump truck, had the right attitude, when its spokesperson Sam Biederman explained the reason for removing the statue thus: "New York City Parks stands firmly against any unpermitted erection in city parks, no matter how small."

These naked Trump statues reflect what author/sociologist Gini Graham Scott, Ph.D., has been pointing out for the past six months in a series of seven books about Trump, now featured on the Website: Trump Is a Nut (http://www.trumpisanut.com), also known as Trump Is Nuts (http://www.trumpisnuts.net) and Who Is Trump Really? (http://www.whoistrumpreally.com). According to the media, Trump is livid and going nuts over these naked images of himself – or maybe he is already nuts, as Scott suggests in a tongue-in-cheek cartoon book *Trump Is Nuts!* The book compares Trump to a series of nuts from peanuts to pecans and shows him ending up in a nut case with two other noted dictators – Hitler and Mussolini, and finally he is hauled off to a nut house. While one of the images shows him regally dressed as an emperor, the naked Trump statues show that underneath the trappings of luxury and royalty, the emperor has no clothes. The *Trump Is Nuts!* book is on Amazon and Kindle, while the cartoons are featured in a video on Pivotshare. They are also part of a trilogy called *Who Is Trump, Really?*

Now, as the popular enthusiasm for the statues shows, more and more people are recognizing in Trump's latest rants that he really is nuts. Some recent examples – and there are so many of them -- are his attack on the American intelligence community, his claim that the 50 military leaders who rejected him as a Commander in Chief are mere has-beens, his comment that a gun going off at a rally could be someone shooting Obama, and his call on Second Amendment supporters to do something to stop Hillary from getting rid of the Second Amendment (actually a false statement), which many viewed as a sly suggestion that someone should assassinate Hillary. But then Trump suggested he was really being sarcastic, or maybe he wasn't. In other words, his words could mean anything, meaning that they really mean nothing.

Or could Trump's crazy words and behaviors be due to the onset of Alzheimer's? It's a question raised by Dr. Gini Graham Scott in an article on the Huffington Post, which has already gotten 1.3 thousand likes and has led to extended discussions on Facebook. http://tinyurl.com/z64hltk. In the article, Scott cites numerous experts, authorities, and writers who have suggested that one reason for Trump's crazy behavior is that he has early-stage Alzheimer's. In fact, they point to him having a half-dozen of the 10 core signs of Alzheimer's, according to the Alzheimer's Association. Plus the condition has genetic links, and Trump's father had Alzheimer's for six years before he died of pneumonia in 1999.

In any event, the naked Trump statues are a fitting "tribute" to a Trump who is increasingly being revealed nationally and internationally for who he really is. In fact, regardless of the many polls which report many different results, the gamblers who take bets are now viewing the odds of Trump winning as going down, down, down. In fact, one of the top polling sites, Nate's Silver's FiveThirtyEight.com has now caught up with the betting sites, giving Clinton a 86.4 percent chance of winning the election, with Trump at 13.6 percent. Now with the statues out there – or perhaps just in millions of shared images – maybe Trump's odds are even less, while the odds of him dropping out of the election are going up, up, up.

ABOUT THE AUTHOR AND ILLUSTRATOR

Gini Graham Scott - Author

Gini Graham Scott has published over 50 books with mainstream publishers, focusing on social trends, work and business relationships, and personal and professional development. Some of these books include *Scammed* and *Lies and Liars: How and Why Sociopaths Lie and How to Detect and Deal With Them.*

She has published over 100 books through Changemakers Publishing, which specializes in self-help, business, and social trends. She has recently launched a line of children's books through Changemakers Kids. She also helps clients write, publish, and promote their books, and has helped dozens of clients find publishers and agents.

She has gained extensive media interest for previous books, including appearances on *Good Morning America, Oprah, Montel Williams, CNN,* and hundreds of radio shows. She is often quoted by the media and has websites at www.ginigrahamscott.com and www.changemakerspublishingandwriting.com. She has about 45,000 listings in Google Search Results.

She has been a regular Huffington Post blogger since December 2012 and has a Facebook page at www.facebook.com/changemakerspublishing. These stories about the election first appeared as Huffington Post blogs.

She has written, produced, and sometimes directed over 60 short videos, which are featured on her Changemakers Productions website at www.changemakersproductions.com and on YouTube at www.youtube.com/changemakersprod.

Her screenplays, mostly in the drama, crime, legal thriller, and sci-fi genres, include several now in distribution or release, including *Suicide Party #Save Dave, Driver, Death's Door,* and *Infidelity.*

She has a PhD in sociology from U.C. Berkeley and MAs in anthropology, pop culture and lifestyles, recreation and tourism, and mass communications and organizational/consumer/audience behavior from Cal State, East Bay. She is getting an MA in communications there in 2017.

Nick Alexander - Illustrator

Writer/artist Nick Alexander was born and raised in New Jersey in a boating family. His first short story was published at the age of 14 in a national magazine. He has since written stage and screenplays, some of which have won awards and been produced and numerous short stories. His traditionally published novels include historical fiction, fantasy. and science fiction. His illustrations have appeared in various publications from children's picture books to political cartoons in newspapers and online. He presently resides outside Sedona, Arizona.

CHANGEMAKERS PUBLISHING
3527 Mt. Diablo Blvd., #273
Lafayette, CA 94549
www.changemakerspublishing.com
(925) 385-0608 . changemakers@pacbell.net

www.ingramcontent.com/pod-product-compliance
Lightning Source LLC
Chambersburg PA
CBHW081152020426
42333CB00020B/2484